AMANDA E. BJERKE

Opening Your Eyes

Becoming Self-Aware as a Young Adult in the 21st Century

First published by Amanda E. Bjerke 2021

Copyright © 2021 by Amanda E. Bjerke

All rights reserved. No part of this publication may be reproduced, stored or transmitted in any form or by any means, electronic, mechanical, photocopying, recording, scanning, or otherwise without written permission from the publisher. It is illegal to copy this book, post it to a website, or distribute it by any other means without permission.

Although the author and publisher have made every effort to ensure that the information in this book was correct at press time, the author and publisher do not assume and hereby disclaim any liability to any party for any loss, damage, or disruption caused by errors or omissions, whether such errors or omissions result from negligence, accident, or any other cause.

Adherence to all applicable laws and regulations, including international, federal, state and local governing professional licensing, business practices, advertising, and all other aspects of doing business in the US or any other jurisdiction is the sole responsibility of the reader and consumer.

The events and conversations in this book have been set down to the best of the author's ability, although some names and details have been changed to protect the privacy of individuals. Neither the author nor the publisher assumes any responsibility or liability whatsoever on behalf of the consumer or reader of this material. Any perceived slight of any individual or organization is purely unintentional.

The resources in this book are provided for informational purposes only and should not be used to replace the specialized training and professional judgment of a physical health care or mental health care professional.

Neither the author nor the publisher can be held responsible for the use of the information provided within this book. Please always consult a trained professional before making any decision regarding treatment of yourself or others.

For more information, email iamamandaevelyn@gmail.com or visit www.openingyoureyes.org

First edition

ISBN: 979-8-9853915-1-0

Cover art by 100 Covers
Editing by The Clever Editors

This book was professionally typeset on Reedsy.
Find out more at reedsy.com

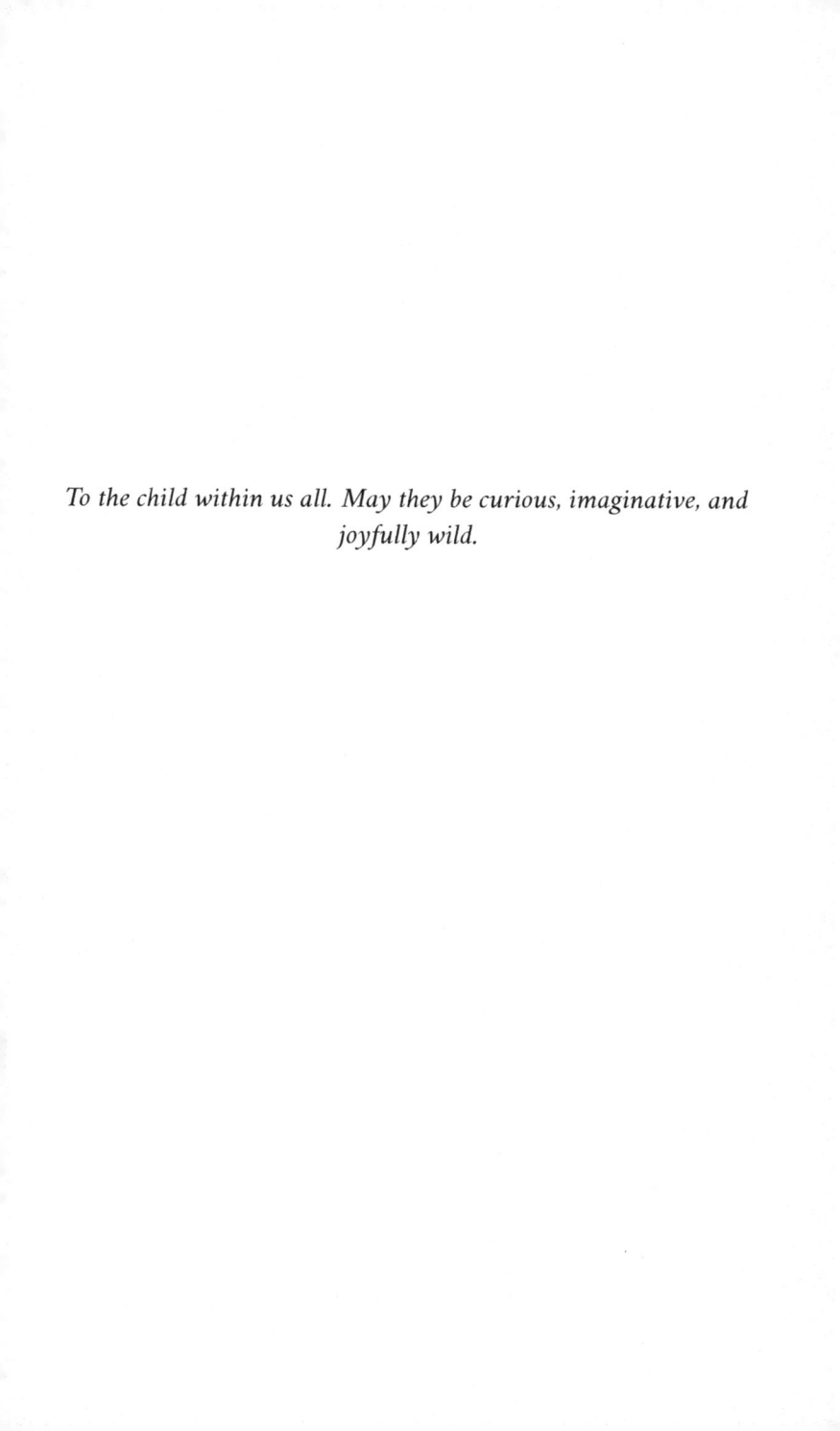

To the child within us all. May they be curious, imaginative, and joyfully wild.

Contents

Acknowledgement   iii
Introduction   v

I   INNOCENCE

1	CHAPTER ONE	3
2	CHAPTER TWO	16
3	CHAPTER THREE	28
4	CHAPTER FOUR	38

II   ANSWERING THE CALL

5	CHAPTER FIVE	53
6	CHAPTER SIX	58
7	CHAPTER SEVEN	65
8	CHAPTER EIGHT	75

III   SHEDDING LAYERS

9	CHAPTER NINE	91
10	CHAPTER TEN	101
11	CHAPTER ELEVEN	114
12	CHAPTER TWELVE	125

IV EMBRACING UNCERTAINTY

13	CHAPTER THIRTEEN	137
14	CHAPTER FOURTEEN	147
15	CHAPTER FIFTEEN	157
16	CHAPTER SIXTEEN	172

V METAMORPHOSIS

17	CHAPTER SEVENTEEN	183
18	CHAPTER EIGHTEEN	194
19	CHAPTER NINETEEN	203
20	CHAPTER TWENTY	212

Citations	218
Leave a Review!	219
About the Author	220

Acknowledgement

I would like to express my sincerest gratitude to the following people who contributed their energy and inspiration into making this book possible:

Thank you to Self-Publishing School for providing me with a solid foundation, road map, and support system that helped turn my dream of being a published author into a reality. Specifically, I'd like to thank Dillon Barr for getting me started with SPS, Scott Allan for offering insightful feedback as a mentor, and Sean Summer and Chandler Bolt for facilitating a wonderful online community of compassionate authors.

Thank you to Christine Driver with the Clever Editors for spending time with me going over edits and answering all of my long-winded questions. Your compassionate, constructive criticism helped me transform my manuscript into something I am so proud of, and your efficiency is unmatched.

Thank you to 100 Covers for the beautiful cover design. I had a vision in my head before finishing this book of what the cover would look like, and they really brought it to life with this artwork.

Thank you to my dearest friend, Cassidy for listening to me ramble until I could properly articulate my thoughts, for reading through snippets and rough drafts of my writing, and for always holding space for me to be my most authentic self. You have changed my life and given my hope for the future.

Thank you to my parents, sisters, and family for giving me unconditional love and making all of this possible in the first place. I am so proud to have you in my corner, and I hope that our relationship grows stronger as we continue on this journey of life together.

Thank you to my teachers, mentors, and colleagues for sharing your wisdom and spirit with me, specifically, Brittany and Jennifer. You have inspired me more than I can express with words, and I truly do not know who I would be today without having met you.

Thank you to the many other remarkable humans who I am lucky enough to call my friends. Your loving presence (whether physical, digital, or spiritual) throughout the process pushed me to keep going. I am so grateful that our paths crossed in this lifetime because experiencing it with you makes me feel alive.

Thank you to Lilly Singh, Haley Hoffman Smith, Kalyn Nicholson, Lindsey Hughes, Zoe Sugg, Ashley Lynn, and so many more incredible women for truly being an outstanding source of inspiration to me for so many years. While I only know most of you through your content on social media, you have genuinely changed my perspective on living a happy life.

Last, but definitely not least, **thank you to the little girl within my heart** for never giving up on yourself. I am incredibly proud of your curiosity, courage, perseverance, compassion, and strength to follow your heart and create this beautiful life.

Introduction

After 22 years of being on this planet, I often think about how the human experience is a unique mystery that our curious species has been trying to understand, articulate, and express throughout the course of our evolution. Our place and purpose in this world, and the universe at large, has baffled generations for millennia. Through research, reflection, and action, we have created, adapted, and destroyed societies and ways of living; yet it seems that the intention and purpose of our existence remains the greatest topic of individual contemplation. Who am I, where am I, how did I get here, and why am I here? These are questions I often ask myself.

When I look back on my life until this point, there are many moments that have made me who I am today. In the greater context of life and my place on this planet, I see the similarities and differences between my own human experience and that of many others around the world. I'm writing this book in the year 2021, and if you've lived through these past few years, you know how much of a rollercoaster ride it's been—to put it nicely. The greatest lesson that I've learned in the past year is that everyone truly is living their own unique human experience that ultimately affects the experiences of others around them. Our individual perceptions impacts how we interact within this world. In the past year, I've spent a great deal of time reflecting on and healing from my past, acknowledging and taking account of my present, and working towards building a durable foundation for my future. This book is a manifestation of that time period. But I understand that for you, your experience has been very different—regardless of when you are reading this.

I feel in my soul that there is another person out there who needs to hear my story, even if that person is simply the younger version of myself. There is another person who has felt what I'm feeling. I don't have to feel alone, and neither do you—a hard lesson to learn. There's beauty in knowing that others can relate to and understand your experience. I believe that there is no greater love than the love you have for yourself, but when you are able to share that love with others, you empower them to find it within themselves too.

I am sure that as I continue to create new memories and go through more challenging experiences, the ones I share in this book may gradually feel smaller and less significant; they may not be as emotionally charged, hold less weight, and potentially lose relevance. I suppose the factual aspect of them happening won't go away, but they may not feel as intense as the years go by and time contributes to my healing.

***

Before I continue, I'd like to briefly write about how our language is limited by the use of dualities such as "good" or "bad," "positive" or "negative," even "young" or "old." Self-awareness is understanding that your individual perception of the use of these words may differ from others.' As humans, we categorize things using the dichotomy of being one thing or another. I feel that our language hasn't evolved enough to fully articulate the complexity of our thoughts and experiences. That being said, when I use words like these, I use them subjectively. Your experience may be different.

***

When I was a child, I was raised to be a "good" kid. I was bright and did very well in school. I was nice to others, well-behaved, and I didn't question or protest much outwardly. While being raised this way was not exactly intentional, it was effective; and it led me to be very aware of my surroundings. I have been observing and taking note of the way people interact and respond to different scenarios and events. One could say that for the majority of my life, I have been a sponge collecting information as if it were water filling up my brain.

In 8th grade, I learned about rocks, space, geology, and other topics in earth science. This is a subject that fascinates me to this day: to think about how beyond our planet, there are hundreds of thousands of other planets and rocks floating through the abyss of space, all interacting and shaping the universe around us, not to mention the possibility of other life forms. There's one specific memory that I have from this science class that has been ingrained in my mind since the day it happened—a memory that has ultimately been the catalyst for writing this book.

***

One day, we are taking notes in class, and Mr. J. asks us a question that is related to a topic we were just assessed on. As he's waiting for someone to raise their hand and answer his question, I notice him glancing over at me. It is about halfway into the school year, and up until this point, I have gotten 100% on every science test we've had.

After about 30 seconds, no one raises their hand. He looks at me and says, "Amanda, you cannot be a sponge, only taking in information. If you know something that others do not, you ought to share it."

***

At the time, I understood what he'd said to mean that I needed to raise my hand and participate more in class. But as I have grown older, I have learned many lessons. I have traveled and learned more about the world, as well as my place in it. I have had many amazing opportunities that others dream to have in their own lives. I say this not to brag or flaunt the privilege that has enabled me to have these experiences. What I mean to say, is that it does not feel right to keep it to myself and not share what I can with others. Of course, there are aspects of my life and experience that no one else will know or understand; but if you can learn from or resonate with something from my story, I hope it is this: we all have a story that is individual and unique to us, yet ultimately, it is a small part of the greater design and larger community. I will never claim to understand all the intricacies of this life; however, my intention in sharing some stories of my own is to show you how these intricacies can transform your perspective. You have experiences within your own life that have transformed you into who you are as you read this. How did you get here? Who has been a part of the journey?

When I began writing this book, I did not know how to express all that I have learned because I had not fully processed it within myself. While I have been taking in information for the past 22 years of my life, self-expression has been something that I have struggled with for many reasons, and that I will talk about that in the next couple chapters. Through the process of writing, I have allowed myself to shine a light on the darker parts of my past, to understand how I came to be in this moment. It has been a long and difficult journey that is far from over, but it has also been the most rewarding adventure I have ever been on.

I have learned that one aspect of expressing yourself comes from first learning how to love yourself for all that you are. On this journey, I have discovered what it truly feels like to love who I am and all that comes with that. I believe it will be an ongoing process as I grow older, but I have learned how to express myself in ways that felt impossible before. This has been the key to releasing the wealth of information that I have been soaking up for all these years. And that is what I want to share with you, as I share my reflections on many influential and foundational experiences from my past.

I wrote this book first and foremost to myself and for the little girl inside me who needed to be seen, cared for, and heard. She deserved to be loved in the way that she loves herself now, and it is no one's fault that she didn't always receive that love, because she didn't know how to communicate it. Now that that she has grown older, it is time to express how she feels and what she needs.

I also wrote this book to you specifically—the person reading this—because like me, you too have your own inner child who has experienced so much that they you may not have understood when you were a kid. Your life is important, and anyone who says otherwise has not felt that same love and compassion for themselves that I want to express to you as you read this. This book is a reminder to anyone who needs it that your existence has an impact on this world and the people in your life. Our world is changing simply because you are living in it, and there is great power in realizing that you can impact so many people with seemingly small and insignificant actions. We are building our future together.

I wrote this book to all of the 20-something-year-olds who feel lost in the transition to adulthood, because wow, is this shit hard, and it didn't come with an instruction manual. There are so many aspects of growing up that I felt like I wasn't prepared for, and I know I am not alone in that. Especially being a young adult in the 21st century, so much has changed since our parents and grandparents were our age, and life is continuing to change at a sometimes alarmingly fast rate. This is by no means a guide to growing up, but I hope that it can help another 20-something-year-old find peace in knowing that it is 100% okay to not have any clue what they are doing with their lives at this point. I promise you, none of us have it all figured out—some of us are just better at faking it until we make it.

I wrote this book to my parents, teachers, elders, etc. to reflect and give thanks for the wisdom they have given me, and to share my perspective, as a young adult in the 21st century. Your wisdom has impacted my life more than you will ever know, and I hope that you can continue to offer your perspective on what you have learned that I may not have yet. I want to make it clear that "young" is a subjective word that is not limited on the basis of age, because there are many people who are still young at heart, well into their seventies, eighties, and nineties.

Finally, I wrote this book to anyone with a dream that they want to make a reality. The concept of "dreams" and a "life purpose" is something that I will talk about in a later chapter. I wrote many chapters of this book while preparing to move to Germany for a year to live out a dream that I have had for a long time, one that I didn't always know was possible until I started taking action on turning it into my reality. I am from the

United States, and in this country, there are so many systems and rules in places that make it more difficult for people to achieve their dreams. I understand that there is great privilege that comes with any opportunity one has in this country, but that should not discredit the power you have to make changes in your life that allow you to work towards actualizing your goals. We cannot always change or control our circumstances, but we can learn to control how we respond and react to them.

If I can help even one person heal or feel seen, then my purpose in publishing this book, rather than filing it away, has been realized. I may not have been alive for very long, but this is what I have learned so far in the past 22 years of my life. I do not claim to know everything; in fact, I often question if I know anything at all. But what I can say is that I am happy, and I feel excited about life. If the lessons I have learned that have gotten me to this point can teach you anything, let it be that you are the only person who can absolutely control how you perceive your life. There is great power and the potential for change in that. There is also great love, but great fear in that as well. Much of what I share in this book has not been easy for me to endure, but I believe that it is an important reflection of the people, places, and experiences that I have encountered in this life.

***

Another crucial clarification I feel is important to include within the introduction of this book is acknowledging the privilege and generational wealth (e.g. being given a vehicle or receiving financial help to buy one) that has made many of the experiences I will share possible. This is something that I am aware of, and I am continuously learning how to support and provide resources to people who may not have access to the same opportunities. Throughout this book, you will notice themes of "learning" and "teaching" because education is something that I am passionate about. Education is power. Currently, I am working as a teacher, but I feel that there is still so much more that I need and would like to learn.

From the outside, I may appear to be an average person, but my experience has not been average. While my family has struggled with finances in the past, the financial stability we have had is more than most. Socioeconomic status plays an incredibly large role in the freedom one has to pursue financial opportunities that raise their social status. Academic performance and one's ability to attend college are also closely linked with this status, even though they are not necessarily accurate measures of a person's intelligence or capability to be happy. I describe the events that, upon reflection, helped me become more self-aware. This process can be more difficult for people who do not have access to the same resources as me, and they may face more obstacles financially.

In relation to financial stability and generational wealth, prioritizing mental health is not always an option for those who are limited by their financial circumstances. Factors such as being the sole income to a family with independents, relying on health insurance through a job, and not having friends, relatives, or credit to draw financial support from make it more difficult to prioritize mental health. In my circumstances, there are variables that exist for me that may not exist for someone else.

This does not discredit the hard work that I or my family have done to get to where we are, but it is an explanation as to how I got here when I did. At this point of my life, I don't know if I am in a place to give advice on specific circumstances that I have not experienced; however, being cognizant of how our circumstances influence the opportunities available to us is crucial in understanding the realities of others. At the end of the day, I'm here to share my experience, and I want to be honest about it. All this being said, it is not my intention to invalidate the very real struggles that people face due to their socioeconomic situation.

**

My story began with being an only child…for about two years. Then my sister came along, and eventually two more sisters. Between me and my youngest sister, there are ten years, a whole decade of life, which has opened my eyes to new ideas and ways of thinking. Not only does this mean that I get to be the annoying older sibling who endlessly stirs the pot, but I also get to share my words of "wisdom" as my sisters go through the years that I have grown out of. We have been through a lot together, but as we continue to grow older, there will be a lot that we go through on our own. Many people would probably agree that we are all quite different from one another, and that we are each our own distinct character, but there are things that we have experienced that will bond us together for the rest of our lives. I will describe this in more depth later in this section, but what I want to express here is that my sisters have taught me how to show compassion, empathy, and above all, taught me what it means to unconditionally love another human being unconditionally.

I believe that connection with other human beings is one of our basic needs. But I also believe that at some point in our lives, we have all felt lonely or have felt truly alone. Especially after 2020, where most of us spent more time by ourselves than we maybe ever did in the past, I see a world that is trying so desperately to heal and to feel loved.

I cannot ever claim to know everything, and I am by no means saying that I know what is best for you in your personal situation—that would be naive and ignorant of me to do so. But what I am saying is that your healing may look different than mine and that is absolutely okay. The important point is that you make the time for yourself to take a step back from your life and assess any areas where you may be wounded or hurting and that need your love and attention.

At the end of each chapter, I have included a series of "Questions to Contemplate" that you can use to do this assessment. For me personally, meditating, journaling, and channeling my emotions into what I create has been a transformative practice for my own healing. For you, this may look different, and that is why I chose the word "contemplate." To contemplate something is to take a thorough look at or think deeply and at length about something. Sometimes, the answers to these questions will flow through your mind the second you finish reading the question; and other times, you may have to sit with these questions in your head for a few hours, days, or even weeks before you are able to articulate your thoughts. Allow yourself that time and space to do so; there is not a timer on how long it *should* take you to heal. I also encourage you to look into further resources that can guide and outline a plan more specific to your individual needs.

This book will not solve all of your problems, but I hope that it serves as a reminder that you have everything you need inside of you to begin solving them on your own. You have been dealt this hand of cards in the game of Life, and some are born with a "better" hand than others; but regardless of the hand you have been dealt, life is hard. It comes with its own unique challenges and obstacles, but I promise you that if you are reading this today, you have survived every challenge you have faced thus far. If you are facing a challenge right now that feels impossible to overcome and you feel like giving up, please, try again and give it all that you've got. Never give up on yourself.

This may be common knowledge, but from living my own experience and watching my sisters, friends, family members, and even complete strangers live their lives, I see that so many people are unconsciously impacted by things that happened to them at a previous time in their life. These unconscious influences can manifest in a variety of ways, but more often than not, I see it manifest into unhappiness, insecurity, jealousy, fear, and overall frustration with life.

For the longest time, I was afraid to share my story and open myself up to the scrutiny perception of others. I believe there are aspects of our identity that we may not share with every person in our lives, nor do we have to. There are many aspects of myself that many of my friends and family may never see. At one point in my life, I kept parts of myself hidden out of fear of judgment. A fear of judgment and a fear of failure have been the dominating fears of my life—as I imagine they are for many, especially in the 21st century where social media places a filter on the ups and downs of our individual realities. There is a beautiful quote credited to Marianne Williamson that goes:

Our deepest fear is not that we are inadequate. Our deepest fear is that we are powerful beyond measure. It is our light, not our darkness, that most frightens us.

There is a fear raging within humanity of our own potential, of our own power. If I am lucky enough to live for many more decades, I know that I will continue to learn and there will always be more that I do not know. However, there is one thing that I am certain of, and that is this: only you are in control of your perception of the power others hold over you. So, I am taking control of my perception of that power and squeezing out the sponge that is my mind to share with you this story. Reflecting on the questions at the end of each chapter, I hope you begin to see the power within yourself. Thank you for being alive today; I am so proud of you for continuing to live and create your own story.

Questions to Contemplate:

1. **Why was I attracted to reading this book? What stood out to me?**
2. **What memories from my past are important to who I am today? Make a list. Think big and small.**
3. **How do I perceive myself? What words would I use to describe myself?**

I

INNOCENCE

1

CHAPTER ONE

"Open your eyes, Amanda," says my mom as she leans closer to me, "You need to open your eyes for me to put the drops in them so that the eye doctor can see what's wrong."

"But I don't want to Mom, it hurts," I tell her as I quiver in my chair.

"It'll be quick. If you open your eyes, I will count to three and put the drops in. And then, just like that," *she snaps* "It'll be over!"

I hesitantly say, "Okay, fine."

I open my eyes and my mom starts counting to three. She puts the first drop in my left eye. It starts to burn and my eyes water. I shut my eyes tightly as tears stream down my cheeks. With all of the willpower in my tiny five-year-old body, I open my eyes again, and my mom puts the last drops in my other eye. Then, I hear a knock on the door.

"Hi Amanda. My name is Dr. X., and I'm going to be taking a closer look at your eyes today. I see you and your mom were able to put the drops in your eyes. How did it go?" asks the ophthalmologist.

I don't say more than a word or two.

"It was a little tricky and uncomfortable, right Amanda?" suggests my mom.

"Yea," I whisper as the doctor begins talking again.

"It can feel kind of weird the first couple of times. I have found that if you try to keep blinking after putting the drops in, it is a little trick to make the sting go away faster."

My mom looks towards me and suggests, "We'll have to try that next time, won't we?"

I nod.

"We put the drops in your eyes to help dilate them. When we dilate the eyes, this helps eye doctors like me to be able to see a better picture of what's going on inside them. So, what do you think? Do you wanna see some really cool pictures of your eyes?"

***

When I was a little girl, my parents took me to see an ophthalmologist; and after many appointments with specialists who dilated and took scans of my eyes, they diagnosed me with Ocular Albinism. Ocular Albinism is a rare genetic condition in the eyes that impacts my vision and depth perception. In the back of my eyes, I am missing a pigment that is necessary for normal vision. My retinas, the light-sensitive part of the eye, are also smaller. Because of this, my eyes constantly shake back and forth as they are trying to focus on what they are perceiving (these uncontrollable repetitive movements of the eye are called nystagmus). This inability to focus and properly take in light affects my depth perception and overall vision. After being diagnosed, I began wearing glasses when I was five years old.

CHAPTER ONE

As early as 1st grade, I had to learn to advocate for myself and my education. In school, I remember having to ask and remind my teachers to put me in the front of the room so that I could see the board. They were also encouraged to use black or blue markers when possible because those were easier colors for my eyes to pick up. I believe that I may have needed official accommodations for my vision through special education in the form of an IEP (Individualized Education Plan). However, from my understanding, I did not receive any, nor was I assessed for them. I know my parents wanted me to feel like a normal kid, but I also believe that it may have been less anxiety-inducing if I would have had outlined accommodations and support mechanisms. Instead, my teachers relied on me to voice my specific needs if I was struggling, but I didn't always know what I needed.

***

Driving to my grandparents' house, our car passes harvested corn fields, tiny farmhouses surrounded by open land, and sporadic housing developments that become more common as you get closer to town. My mom is driving, as my dad comments from the passenger seat, and my three younger sisters and I stare out the windows. My grandparents live only a few miles away from our house, but the drive is the same every time, so it feels farther away than it is.

My dad turns around in his seat and asks my sisters and I, "Girls, do you know what road we are coming up to?" Nina and I are the oldest; I am a freshman in high school, and she is in 6th grade. I know my dad is asking this question because I am going to be learning how to drive soon.

I say, "No."

"County Road 19," Nina says.

"Nice! Amanda, how don't you know this yet? We go to grandma and grandpa's house the same way every time. Don't you pay attention?" responds my dad.

They've asked me these kinds of questions before, and each time their response is the same. If he would have asked me which direction to turn at the intersection, I would have told them to turn right. What my family seems to always forget is that I have Ocular Albinism which impairs my vision and makes it difficult for me to read street signs.

***

This is something that I was born with, and I have had to learn to adapt and live with the challenges and obstacles it has created in my life. I am not able to see very far or clearly without my glasses. When my parents would ask me what road we were coming up to, I didn't know the answer because for my entire life, it had been difficult for me to clearly read the road signs we passed. I know that I shouldn't have felt ashamed for not knowing what road we were driving up to, but the way my family responded to my answer each time instilled shame in me. *How did they understand my eye disorder? Did they understand how much it truly impacted me growing up? Did they ever forget that my eyesight is drastically worse than most people's?* They told me that I didn't pay attention, so I felt like I didn't pay attention. They told me I needed to be aware of my surroundings, so I felt like I hadn't been aware of my surroundings. It felt as if they were putting blame on me for something that I could not control. My vision and eye disorder were literally caused by them—it is a *genetic* condition—yet I felt like I did something wrong.

As I got older and started learning how to drive, I realized that all my life, I had believed that I was "directionally challenged." I had been told over and over that I was bad at directions, and this was a problem. Driving and my eyes have a complex, intertwined relationship in my mind, which I will describe more in depth in Chapter 6.

***

When I was in high school, I began learning more about the scientific aspects of my eye disorder in a public speaking class. For one of our assignments, we had to give an informative speech, and I decided that I wanted to give one about Ocular Albinism. This was a great learning opportunity for me because even though it was something that I had been living with for years, I did not know a lot about what it actually was biologically or genetically. I researched the history of the disorder and the specifics of how this genetic mutation occurs in the eye as it develops. But in the last section, I also described a little bit about my personal experience with it and how it impacted my daily life.

On the day of giving my speech, I was excited to share with my peers about something so personal to my experience. I gave my speech, and my classmates began asking me questions. One of my peers asked, "So if you're basically almost blind, does that mean you are technically disabled or that you have a disability?" This is a question that I have struggled with for my entire life.

The general definition from the Centers for Disease Control and Prevention (CDC) of a "disability" is a condition that limits a person's abilities or makes it more difficult for them to effectively interact with people or the world around them. My eyes shake back and forth, so people can usually tell that something is different about me. When I was younger, I grappled with the idea of myself being "disabled" due to my eye disorder and blurred vision because at the time, the only representation I had seen of a person with a disability related to their vision was someone who is blind and walking with a cane.

My parents wanted me to live as normal of a life as possible, so they did not put much emphasis on my eye disorder or consider how much it may have impacted my daily life. This was both a blessing and a curse for me because it allowed me to grow up feeling like I was not limited by my disorder; however, it did, and does, greatly impact my daily life. That being said, I didn't always feel like I was able to communicate those struggles to the people around me.

When I was a child, it was hard for me to describe my eye disorder and the way I saw the world to people. It was also difficult sometimes to convey when I was struggling. I wouldn't say I was ashamed of my eye disorder, but it was a topic I avoided talking about. I was able to advocate for myself when necessary in school, but it was never the center of anyone's attention. At home, my family didn't seem to quite understand the limitations of my vision, so I never felt comfortable asking for or expressing that I needed help. At school, I was never bullied for my eye disorder or the fact that my eyes shake back and forth—at least, not to my face or knowledge—but it was something my peers could definitely notice. When you are younger, and especially in middle and high school, it feels like any difference you have is a potential target for someone to attack. For a long time, my eyes were an insecurity of mine. Therefore, besides my ophthalmologist, my lack of vision was something not many people truly understood the extent of. Looking back, this made it very difficult for me to identify the extent of my visual impairment.

Because of the significant impact my eye disorder has on my ability to function in my daily life, I would now answer that student's question by saying, "Yes, to an extent, I have a disability." I struggled with coming to this conclusion for a long time because I know that there are people who have disabilities that impact their lives more significantly than mine impacts me. This line of thinking was very damaging for me because it invalidated my own experiences and struggles. Depending on the degree of vision a person with Ocular Albinism has, it may not be a disability for them because it effects each person's vision differently. With the degree of vision that I have, I have come to terms with its significant impact on my life. Not only have I learned more about my disorder on a scientific level, but I have also learned more about it on a personal level. To do this, I had to take a look back at many situations in my life where my eyesight created a conflict or difficulty in my life.

***

One memory that comes to mind immediately was a conversation I had with two of my volleyball coaches at the end of our Junior Varsity season, in my junior year of high school. We were discussing how I felt the season went and what my goals were for the future. Throughout the season, I felt that these coaches were not very supportive or constructive in the criticism they gave me, which honestly, made me hate playing the sport entirely. Because of how they treated me and my other teammates, this was probably the last time that I was going to play volleyball competitively.

Despite this, I was grateful to have had the opportunity to play a sport that I had loved for so long. When I was first diagnosed with Ocular Albinism, the doctors told my parents that there was a good chance that I would not be able to play any sports or drive a car because of my vision and depth perception; so I was happy that I was able to play as long as I did. I decided in that conversation to share my gratitude and how proud of myself I was. I think about halfway through telling them this story, I realized that I had never talked in depth with them about my eye disorder before because their expressions changed dramatically. When I finished talking, they both said that they had no idea about how much it impacted my ability to play the sport, but they were proud that I stuck it out as long as I did. Up until this point, these coaches did not know the extent to which my eye disorder impacted my depth perception, which ultimately impacted how I played, but I did notice that their feedback became more constructive after I explained it to them.

If you look closely and notice fine details, you will notice that there is something different about my eyes; but if it's not something you are paying attention to, you may not know that there's anything different. If the priority was to win every game, then I understand why the coaches chose to play other girls instead of me, because I was not the best on the team. They did not know about my visual impairment for the majority of the season, so I couldn't really blame them for not being understanding. That being said, their coaching and how they went about giving me feedback during practices over the course of those years playing volleyball in high school, regardless of having a disability or not, was disappointing. Despite losing the love I once had for the sport because of that harsh criticism, playing volleyball taught me a valuable lesson: if you believe it is possible, and I mean if you honestly *believe* it, then it is possible. If you *believe* that it is not possible, then it won't be. Persevering despite being told that I wouldn't be able to play sports was the only option I had if I wanted to play.

Since then, I have taken time to process the mental and emotional impact of having Ocular Albinism. As an adult, my perspective has changed, and I have realized how much of a blessing it has been. It made me the person I am today. The way that I literally see impacts my perspective on life more than I realized as a kid.

***

In college, I began to contemplate the metaphorical and philosophical aspect of "vision" in relation to "perspective." To be clear, I am not blind. It has long been a challenge for me to describe exactly how I see the world in comparison to others because I cannot see what others see. As I share my story throughout these next few chapters, I'd like you to keep that point in mind. As I know that I may never fully understand your experience, you may never fully understand my own.

Now as a young adult, I have seen how my relationship with my disability has changed. As I mentioned, I am not completely blind, but I have a medically diagnosed eye disorder that has led to me having significantly worse vision than the majority of the global population. It has felt isolating at times, because I don't know many other people who understand the mental toll it takes on an individual to cope with the personalized struggles of living with my disorder. I now understand that my disability is no less valid or real than any other.

I have had to work hard to not let it control the way I interact with the world around me. I have felt subconsciously judged because of my lack of vision, and I have noticed slight differences in the ways people interact with me. I am finally in a state of mind where this doesn't bother me anymore, and I can make light-hearted jokes about my eyesight (or lack thereof). It took a long time for me to find my peace with this part of my identity that I cannot change.

How we perceive the world influences the way we interact in it. Our eyes are one aspect of this perception. They help us to process visuals in our outer reality in order to draw conclusions about the environment around us. We all perceive it differently because our perception is shaped by so many things besides what we literally see. For example, I cannot see tiny details on people's faces, and I rarely can tell what someone's eye color is when I first meet them. But metaphorically, there is so much more that I am able to see about a person besides their physical characteristics.

It wasn't until my early twenties when I finally felt truly comfortable, and even confident in my vision and how I perceived its impact on my life. It was a long journey to get to this point, but I learned a lot of valuable lessons along the way. While my eyes are not the reason or means of how I learned these lessons, I think there is something to be said about how we *see* the lessons in the failures and obstacles that life puts us through.

I was born in 1998 and am on the cusp between being a Millennial and a part of Gen Z. My perception has been greatly influenced by the generational differences between the world in which the Millennials grew up in and the one that Gen Z is growing up in. Even more so, I am writing this book amidst the COVID-19 pandemic, in which everything we once deemed "normal" and "safe" has been flipped on its head.

For centuries, humans have lived in a world without cell

phones, social media, Artificial Intelligence, etc. Those of us on the older end of our generation remember our childhood without so much technology. We quite literally see the world differently than how our parents and grandparents saw the world at our age. That is no disrespect to their perspective, because that wisdom and experience has gotten us to this point. However, we cannot expect the same from young adults now as we did twenty years ago, let alone fifty. That is not to say that our society should expect less. My point is that we need to let go of these expectations all together and come to terms with the fact that we don't need to be confined by other people's expectations of us.

How I live my life is different from how you, the reader, live yours, so why should we be expected to produce the same outcome in terms of the general paths we take?

By some chain of circumstances, you have been brought to this moment, reading this line on the page. Our experiences have been very different, and I acknowledge that there are many factors that influence our circumstances. I have lived my entire life with a perspective drastically different from others, but there are similarities between all of our stories that we can connect to, relate with, and learn from. That is where self-awareness comes in.

In the next chapter, I will share the most influential experience of my entire life, because reflecting on it as an adult made me aware of how much it influenced the way that I perceived my existence to this day. But just because it was the "most influential" experience of my life does not mean that it will have the same impact on you. In fact, there may be parts of my story that do not resonate with you at all or that you do not fully understand, and that is okay. Afterall, self-awareness is about understanding *you*self, as in you the reader, not *my*self, as in me the author.

The "Questions to Contemplate" at the end of each chapter, are meant to be used as a tool to dive deeper into understanding who you are and how you got to this point. When you become aware of how your thoughts and experiences influence your perception of yourself and the world around you, you will begin to see that you have the power to change, create, and live a life that is authentic and fulfilling.

If you are still unsure of how this book can help you, let me be clear: reading this book cannot help you change your life on its own. It can provide inspiration, guidance, encouragement, solidarity, etc. But at the end of the day, it's all you, boo. You are the one who decides how you take action to change and grow as a person. Self-awareness doesn't just show up overnight. It's something you nurture and intentionally build upon as you experience new things, and that it is not an effortless process or an exact science. But if you are:

- **confused about or trying to figure out what to do with your life,**
- **giving up on your dreams and passions,**
- **struggling to find a purpose,**
- **curious to learn more about yourself,**
- **or questioning why you are even here in the first place,**

then please keep reading and contemplating your existence with me. One of the biggest queries our generation currently faces is how to navigate our coming-of-age and adulthood in an era dominated by technology and social media. I promise you, opening your eyes, becoming self-aware, and learning how to love and take care of yourself in the 21st century will be the best things you ever do for *you* in your entire life.

Questions to Contemplate:

1. **What role do the opinions of others play in how I live my life? How do they affect my relationships?**
2. **What aspects of myself do I criticize? What am I insecure about? How does this reflect in the way I look at the world?**
3. **What aspects of my do I hide from the world? Why do I hide or sensor these parts of myself?**

2

CHAPTER TWO

As I became more aware of how my vision impacted my perception of the world, I used art as a way to express how I saw and interpreted it. It started with drawing characters from movies and shows that I liked, and it eventually progressed to sketching and painting scenes around me and from my imagination. It was also a way for me to become comfortable with my vision and how different it was from others. I felt that many did not understand my eye disorder or the impact it had on my life, especially at the time. There were times when I would try to explain how I saw something to someone, and they assumed I meant that the world just looked blurry, but it is much more complicated than that. Even as an adult, it is often hard for me to describe how I see something, because the other person does not have the same frame of reference as I do. Expressing myself artistically was a way for me to share my world with other people when I felt they did not understand, but most of the time, I kept my art to myself. Vibrant colors were especially useful, because I often associated it with my emotional state at the time I was

CHAPTER TWO

creating, and they were the easiest for my eyes to pick up.

Each year, the elementary school in our district would submit student artwork to be displayed at the local library. One year, I had a clay sculpture that was put on display, and I also had a drawing that was in the show the next year. When I was in middle school, most of our art was put on display around the school or in the art room, but it wasn't put out as often for the community to see.

One of my cousins, who is a year younger than me, also really enjoyed art and drawing his favorite cartoon characters. This was something we bonded over when we were younger; and at family get-togethers, we would spend time drawing and sharing our ideas and creativity with one another. He loved attention growing up and, in my opinion, definitely sought it out. He also had a habit of trying to one-up people when they would tell a story. *What made him feel that he needed to do this?* My parents raised me to not seek out the validation or attention of others and or to not brag about myself. Because of that, whenever I had an accomplishment, my parents would be the ones to talk about it with my grandparents and relatives. They would often talk about me right in front of my face, but they rarely asked me questions or spoke to me directly. *What was their perception of me?* This made me feel like I didn't know what I could or could not talk about when it came to how I felt or my accomplishments, because I didn't want to steal the attention away from someone else.

I was raised to be the "nice" and "quiet" girl, and I was often ignored, forgotten, or neglected when it came to being included in conversations with my extended family. Knowing how this was emotionally difficult for me to process as a kid, I didn't want anyone else to feel like they were being silenced or ignored in the way that I was. Despite my cousin wanting to be the center of attention, for a while, creating art was something that we had in common. It was a connection that transcended words and helped us bond with one another. But when I began middle school, that connection changed very quickly.

One year in particular, my cousin had an art piece that was on display in the library, like I had a couple years prior. A relative of my grandma, who is an author of many children's books, poetry, and informative works on farming, was visiting the library with his wife one day. They saw his artwork and were impressed with it. They decided to ask him if he would illustrate their next children's book. Thus, setting the foundation for a psychologically traumatic experience in my childhood.

There had been no talk of a book before then, and I found out at a family get-together when someone told me that he had been chosen to illustrate the book. *How did this make him feel? Did he understand how amazing of an accomplishment this was?* As a child, this hurt me so much because as I mentioned, creating artwork was a tool I used to cope with the anxiety, uncertainty, and insecurity I had with my eye disorder, and my work was something that I was proud of. Struggling to cope with having a disability that many could not understand made this experience extremely damaging to my confidence and self-worth. My cousin was definitely talented, but I often questioned why my artwork wasn't good enough to be asked to illustrate a book or why my family didn't seem to care about how it made me feel. *How did they feel about this opportunity for him? What were they thinking at the time this was happening?*

When he was illustrating for this book, that was all my family seemed to talked about when we were together: how proud they were of him and how good of a job he was doing. Never once did they ask me about my artwork or about what I liked drawing or painting. *Did they know that art was important to me? Did they understand that it was a way for me to cope with my eye disorder?* I hated whenever the topic came up, and I was jealous of him for getting so much attention. The thought of it made me lay in bed at night, crying myself to sleep sometimes.

My grandma would often ask me to go to different events with my cousin and her relatives because she didn't want him to be alone for it all, and she thought that I might enjoy it. And in truth, I did enjoy going to those events with them because in a way, it did help me to feel included. At the same time, it also felt like his *"success"* was being rubbed in my face every single time, because *he* was the one creating the illustrations, not me. *He* was the one being acknowledged for his creativity and creations, not me. *He* was the one that everyone was proud of and wanted to know more about, not me. At an early age, I felt so jealous, because all I could think was "Why wasn't this me?" "Why wasn't I good enough for them to consider?" I held a lot of anger and resentment towards my cousin and my family. I felt very hurt, because it felt like my voice was being ignored or never asked for, let alone appreciated. I felt hurt, because it felt like my family didn't care about what was important to me. I felt hurt, because I didn't understand my emotions at the time or know what to do—I was a child.

As an adult, I've been able to identify these emotions, and I am aware that there were no ill intentions behind my relative's decision to have my cousin illustrate his book. He hadn't seen any of my artwork in the same capacity that he saw my cousin's. But as a child, I did not know or understand that; and no one took the time to talk to me or ask me about how

I was feeling. When a child sits alone with that much pain, anger, and jealousy, that is the breeding ground for emotional trauma.

I remember one day, after the book was published, I was so upset that I took my entire collection of drawings, paintings, and miscellaneous artwork and I threw it all away. As I was throwing each piece into a garbage bag, one by one, the same thoughts kept running through my mind, "Why did you create these in the first place? Who would want to see these anyways? No one else cares about it, so why do you? It isn't even that good." I recognize these thoughts now to be the manifestation of how I felt my family viewed me at the time; but as a child, I honestly thought that was how they felt. That was how I felt, and the jealous and anger ate away at my soul. That experience was emotionally humiliating for me at a young age, and I know how much those thoughts hurt that little girl's heart.

I wanted to be happy for my cousin, because it truly was an amazing opportunity for him, and he did an amazing job creating the illustrations. However, when you see someone else succeeding in something that you are so passionate about, while you're and not receiving any type of acknowledgment, let alone praise, it is easy to have feelings of jealousy and envy. If you sit alone with those feelings long enough, they turn into resentment.

When I was younger, allowing myself to feel those emotions made me feel alone, so I often suppressed them and pushed them as far down as I could so no one else would see them. Thankfully, I have now been able to work through quite a bit of those memories that held so much emotion for a long time, but it still hurts. It took a lot of work on my part, but now, my cousin and I have a healthier relationship and have been able to reconnect. We are now able to encourage and support one another in all of our life's endeavors, but it was not easy for me to get there.

In the first few years of adulthood, I decided that I no longer wanted to feel the way that I did towards him, and I began to shine a light on those shadows that had been kept in the dark since I was in middle school. When I began opening these doors that had been padlocked for almost a decade, it hurt all over again. The anger came flooding back ten times more powerful than when I was a kid, because I remember how much it hurt then, and it hurt me even more to know that nothing had changed within my family. I realized that I felt more anger and resentment towards them than I had felt towards my cousin.

From a more mature perspective, I was able to process that anger. I became more aware of my family's perspective, and I realized that they, of course, never meant to cause me any harm throughout my childhood. I believe that we all have a complicated family history. Somewhere along the line, there is drama. Somewhere along the line, there is the possibility of trauma. But that does not excuse the pain that it causes. Processing these memories allowed me to finally be able to validate that pain, because somewhere along the line, someone has to break the cycle.

I have seen how my parents' relationships with their siblings and my grandparents continue to influence them in adulthood, and how it has also affected the dynamics within our own nuclear family. *Do they see how these relationships impact our family? How do they feel about their relationships with their siblings and parents?* At the end of the day, I know many of the people in my extended family care about me, and I care about many of them. However, when it comes to my own mental health and well-being, I have needed to heal wounds that they created and move on from the toxic patterns that were instilled in them by their parents and their grandparents before them. To this day, much of my extended "family" doesn't talk with my sisters and I when we see them, and there hasn't really been any effort to get to know us. *Why is that? Should I have made the first move to initiate more conversation?* I'm at an age now where I am no longer waiting for them to show interest or compassion towards us. At this point, it has meant cutting most of them out completely or not letting them in at all. Could this change in the future? Maybe, but I'm not gonna hold my breath.

In the end, the only questions I still have—which have been hard for me to process and heal from—are, "Why did no one ask me how I felt? Did they not see me hurting?" I was a child. I did not know any better. I have learned that, while although my family is responsible for their actions and behavior, they did not know any better. The hard part about communicating as a child is that you don't have the vocabulary or comprehension to always fully understand how you are feeling or how to identify what you are feeling. Your parents, and the other adults in your life, may not be responsible for your actions or how you respond in a situation, but they are responsible for teaching you how to communicate and express yourself in healthy ways. If you are not able to do this, it is likely that you will perpetuate a cycle of neglect and feel alone.

Throughout my emotional healing, I have learned that one should not take anything personally in this life. The reason I am telling you these intimate details about my childhood is because I want to show you a glimpse of my roots and to demonstrate that every cause has an effect. Every behavior creates an emotional response. The actions and behaviors of others are a reflection of their relationship with themselves and their perception of the world. In this situation, my family's behavior during that time was not a reflection of how they felt about me. It was a reflection of how they perceived that experience. They were being supportive of my cousin in his well-deserved accomplishments and did not realize that they weren't paying as much attention to me, my sisters, and my other cousins. It took me some time to meditate and reflect on these memories, but I have realized that this jealousy and resentment from my childhood is where my fear of failure and my fear of judgment came from.

***

When I started college, I met a girl named Eleanor in one of my classes. From the moment we met, I somehow knew that this girl and that we would be friends. As we started getting to know one another better, there were many passions and interests that we had in common such as our love of learning German and interest in spirituality. Initially, I was worried that having so many shared interests may negatively impact our friendship because of the experiences I had had in the past with my cousin. But boy, was I wrong. After several years of friendship, I honestly believe that we were destined to meet, because she taught me a lesson that I needed to learn, in order to fully heal from the emotional trauma of my past.

The difference between my experience with my cousin and my experiences with her is I perceive her as being an individual who is living *her* truth first and foremost. My cousin is obviously also an individual, but there were many times when I felt that he was copying me. Because of this, for the longest time, I hated when people would do something similar to me or have a similar specific interest. They say mimicry is a form of flattery, admiration, and respect, but it never felt that way. *Did my cousin intentionally copy me? Was he genuinely interested in the same things I was? Did I take his mimicry the wrong way?* When I was a kid and this happened with other people in school, that person usually got the attention for the shared interest or talent, and it made me feel hidden or forgotten. That was a powerful feeling—to feel forgotten. My cousin has now put down parts of his façade and is now living *his* truth. That initial mimicry always felt like an attempt to silence me, but I these experiences taught me that imitation or mimicry doesn't have to be viewed negatively. Both people can be individuals while still enjoying shared interests.

When you have things in common with people, and especially friends, you can challenge them to be the best versions of themselves, for no one other than themselves. You can believe in your own talent while also believing in the talent of someone else; and you can celebrate your success while simultaneously celebrating the successes of others.

***

Jealousy, envy, and resentment are heavy emotions to live with. They slowly eat away at your joy and steal away the possibility of any connection with that person you have those feelings towards. I share these stories from my life, because I think vulnerability is important in order to build both respect and trust. However, it's also important for me to share these stories because it shows you that I understand what it feels like to be jealous when you see someone else living your dream, or to see someone else doing something that you really want to do in your life. I fear that if people don't open their eyes and take a closer look at how their emotional experiences still influence their emotions today, they will allow themselves to sink into jealousy or resentment and forget that the only person they need to live their life for is themselves.

Social media and the internet will continue to be prevalent parts of our society; and our capabilities for their use are growing seemingly exponentially by the decade. There is so much power in being able to connect with millions of people around the world. The fact that there are over seven billion people on this planet means that the chances of there being somebody out there that likes the same things you do and has similar passions as you do is pretty high. They may even be better at utilizing those passions and skills than you are. There will be people out there who copy the things you do and use your ideas as their own; and it may hurt, but I promise, in some twisted way, it's supposed to be a compliment. You will find people with similarities just as much as you'll find people with differences. That is the beauty of the human experience. Your life is not validated by accomplishments in comparison to others.

There was a lengthy period in my life where I believed that my story was not important and that it did not need to be shared. For the longest time, I had this urge to write about my life and what I have learned, not only from my eye disorder and events in my childhood, but also from the places I am grateful to have traveled to, which I will share in Chapters 9, 10, and 14. I found myself asking, is my message important? Am I really a writer or an artist or a creative person? I was doubting myself because that is how I perceived others felt about me. It was a belief that was rooted in those emotional wounds from my past. I fell victim to the idea that I am defined by those memories, and I was worrying about things that I couldn't control. Finding the root of my insecurity took many years and a lot of reflection and patience. However, it is important for me to share with you how transformative it was for me to take the time to think about how I was raised and how it made me feel growing up.

It is important to acknowledge the younger versions of yourself, and it's also important for you to love them and let them heal. They are just as much a part of you as the current version you are experiencing. Ultimately, every version of you that has come before the one you are now has gotten you to this very moment. That doesn't mean you won't have regrets because I know I certainly do. But if I've learned anything about life, it's that life is a constant cycle of unpredictable ups and downs. If you don't take the time to heal from those difficult moments, you will regret repeating the cycle until you do. And that only makes it harder to see the beauty and opportunity that surrounds you.

I'm not here to tell you how to live your life. I'm not here to diagnose you. I'm not here to say that I know better than you. None of that would be true. I am here to share the experiences that I've had in my life and what I've learned through reflecting on them, in order to grow and become more aware of myself. When I surrendered the guard I had put up for years, I realized that I wasn't defending myself from my family or from another person; I was trying to protect the little girl inside of me from having to see herself throw away everything that was important to her. I tried to ignore these memories for a long time. Eventually, it hurt me more to suppress them. I cannot change the past, but I am responsible for my own healing. The wounds don't exactly go away, and sometimes you have to let them breathe; but when you look that pain in the eye, it is a little less scary to face when it pops back up.

Questions to Contemplate:

1. **How do I express myself?**
2. **What negative experiences or trauma have I let define me? How can I let go of them and reclaim my power?**
3. **What did I need more of as a child?**

CHAPTER THREE

When I was a young child, maybe five or six years old, I remember I did something that was "wrong," and I knew what was going to happen next: my dad was going to spank me, and it was going to hurt. I ran behind the couch and clung onto the railing of our stairs. My mom and dad both kept saying that I needed to come out from behind the couch, because I wasn't going to avoid the spanking either way. I tried to run from behind the couch into my parents' room, but my dad was quicker than me. I learned that trying to fight it made it worse, so I tried to not move. He bent me over his knee and beat my behind until I started crying.

***

When I think back to that memory, I do not remember what I did to deserve that, but I do know that whatever I had done was wrong. I was aware that my dad was going to spank me to punish me for what I did. What I did not understand, at the time, was *why was I going to be punished in that way, if I already understood that it was not okay and that I would not do it again?*

I do not believe that any child deserves to be beaten, ever. People can justify until they are blue in the face that they spank their kids to "discipline" them, but if you were to treat another adult the same way parents use spanking to "discipline" their kids, you would be arrested for assault. So, if it is unacceptable and even against the law to beat a grown adult, why is it acceptable to hit a child in this way?

I know there are many people within my generation and generations before us who experienced this type of upbringing. It is interesting to discuss the concept of discipline with people who grew up differently than I did, because I'm curious to learn about other parenting styles that don't involve spanking. From my experience and listening to the experiences of others, parents justify spanking their kids as "discipline," but oftentimes, it is an emotional response to how they are feeling in the moment and as a result of how they were treated as a kid. A child is young, innocent, and helpless in the power dynamic of parent and child. In my opinion, it is an abuse of power for parents to hit their kids, and it is a sign of emotional immaturity within the parent, regardless of whether it's for the purpose of "discipline."

It is possible for one to simultaneously love and respect their parents, while also disagreeing with or criticizing aspects of how they were raised. One does not necessarily negate the other. I love and respect my parents, because I know that they did the best that they could with the circumstances they had. However, it is important for me to open a conversation about how I disagree with certain aspects of how I was raised. It is important for me to hold this space for the validity of my emotions, as I also believe that it is important for you to hold that space for yourself as well.

My dad is a bit more traditional and old-school than my mom when it comes to parenting and gender roles in the family. This became clearer as I got older, but when I was a kid, it was not something I was fully aware of, because I didn't know anything different. I respect my dad greatly for his work ethic and commitment to our family. He often puts our needs above his own, and I hope that he and my mom will be able to focus more on themselves once all of my sisters and I move out. They deserve to be happy and to have time to reflect once their kids are adults before moving on to the next phases of their lives. In addition to spankings, there have been other moments in my life where I felt he crossed a line.

***

When I was in 7th or 8th grade, my dad, my three sisters, and I went down to the gas station. We were getting gas, and we were allowed to get one treat. One of my sisters had a lot of "tantrums" (as we called them) when she was younger. I now understand that these "tantrums" probably come from a mental illness or disorder, because she could not control them. I don't know which one specifically, because my family hasn't really been proactive on therapy or dealing with any form of mental illness. Among several other reasons, this is primarily due to how my parents were raised growing up on small farms in the Midwest. They didn't have access to the kind of knowledge about mental health and the impact of mental illness that we have today. Anyway, when we went down to the gas station, my sister wanted to get a certain treat and my dad told her no. She started having a tantrum, and my dad was getting visibly mad, because she wouldn't stop. He got embarrassed easily by those kinds of things when they happened in public.

CHAPTER THREE

After taking the treat away from her and paying, we all went out to the car and my dad was yelling at her to stop screaming, but she wouldn't. As soon as we got home, two sisters ran downstairs, and the other ran upstairs, followed by my dad. I came in after him, and what I remember seeing and hearing as I watched from the bottom of the steps, was my dad spanking her harder than I have ever seen someone hit a human being. Even as I write this, I feel remnants of the emotions I felt then, hearing the screaming and crying all over again. *Were my sisters as psychologically impacted as I was? Do they remember this happening?* What my sisters and I experienced that day, especially my sister who was being hit, was trauma. Absolute trauma.

***

It was in these moments and my reflection on them thereafter when I realized that there absolutely is a difference between discipline and abuse. *Why did my dad feel as strongly as he did? Was he taking those emotions out on my sister? What thoughts did he have afterwards? Was he treated this was a child?* In the case of my parents and grandparents, they were raised getting spanked and beaten when they did something wrong; it was very normalized at the time. Parents may have heard their kid screaming or exhibiting behavior that they didn't want, so they resorted to spanking to make it stop. Rather than investigating the cause of the behavior or communicating/demonstrating the appropriate behavior, spanking was used to scare the child into not doing it again. That physical impact leaves an energetic trace on a person for the rest of their lives, and it can make it difficult for the child to communicate with others as they get older.

Therapy hasn't always been easily accessible for me, but

I had to start somewhere, and all I had was myself, time, and a journal. I kept this journal next to me in the event it was easier for me to write my thoughts rather than simply meditate on them, (because sometimes my mind can be a scary place, with some wild intrusive thoughts). I started at the beginning and worked through remembering and visualizing the earliest memories I had. Working through childhood trauma is difficult, especially if you are within close proximity of the place or people who were involved in the trauma. You experience a vast range of emotions when processing it as well. There is guilt, shame, anger, resentment, fear, regret, disappointment, etc. "Trauma" is a word that is often thrown around to express a significant impact something had on one's life, but it is a very real and serious thing that is not to be taken lightly. It manifests differently in every person who experiences it, and it truly impacts you psychologically.

One by one, I began remembering memories from when I was a kid; and as I allowed myself to feel my emotions from those memories, I came to a few conclusions.

What I learned is that the way people treat you is a reflection of how they are treating themselves. Deep down, I feel that my dad hit my sister the way he did because that's what happened to him when he was a kid, and he was raised to believe that he deserved that. No one ever deserves to be beaten or violated like that, period. I don't care what the excuse or "justification" is, it is never okay to lay your hands on another human being like that.

When a parent acts out of anger, it is abuse. Spanking is abuse. You can say that our generation is sensitive and that we are weak but being beaten as a child has significant psychological impacts on their development. Regardless of the "purpose" for the beating, the consequences echo throughout a person's life. I can still hear the screams. I can still feel the pain, even if it was not my own. Continuing that cycle, generation after generation, also has a profound effect on a family.

I think that any time you process trauma, you have to first acknowledge the impact it had on you, especially when it comes to things that happen in your childhood. I will speak more specifically on the topic of forgiveness in a later chapter, but you also need to forgive yourself for doing the best you could, even if it didn't seem like you did enough. You were a child. Our childhood is a vulnerable time period, where our minds and bodies are still developing. You did not know any better. You trusted the people who were supposed to protect you from the dangers of the world. You didn't know that they too would be one of the dangers that you would have to learn to protect yourself and your sisters from.

There may be a lot you have to work through when you get older. You can wait, and you can try to suppress those emotions for as long as you can, but it comes up. It comes up in many different shapes and forms, and it manifests into your life. Any pain, anger, frustration, shame, fear, regret, etc. that you are trying to ignore or push down, will come out eventually, as it did with my father. Allow yourself to cry—crying is the body's expression of healing.

It's hard to work through and process toxic family dynamics and childhood trauma. I chose to write about this early on, because I believe that it is an important part to becoming self-aware and understanding who you are as a person. Many of our habits, insecurities, and mannerisms come from previous generations and the environments we were raised in. When I would think about those situations in my life, my mind would begin to think and tell myself that, "It's not a big deal. You're being dramatic. This happens to every kid. That's how you learn." But the truth is, it is a big deal to me. It shouldn't have to happen to any kid, because that is not the only way to learn. I believe there is such a thing as natural consequences. I don't believe violence is ever the answer when it involves a child.

Something people don't talk enough about is family dynamics and the reasons parents behaved the way they did. As our parents grow older and do their own work to understand themselves and break intergenerational trauma, they too question how they were raised and conditioned to function in our society. It is hard to work through childhood trauma, at any age, because you were a kid when it happened. But I promise you, breaking the cycle is possible. It is hard, and it is scary, but it is not impossible. In the next chapter, I will describe the moment when I was able to break this specific cycle within my immediate family.

***

We are living in a period of time, where I believe we are experiencing a paradigm shift: a major change in how we as humans think, create, and get things done that ultimately challenges and replaces the old ways in which things were done before. We are living in a new century, facing obstacles that will dramatically influence the course of the next one hundred years, such as the climate crisis, the advancement of AI technology, socioeconomic disparities, etc. Younger generations in the US today have grown up in a world where school shootings, terrorist attacks, police brutality, natural disasters, economic collapse, and a global pandemic (to name a few things) are in the foundational experiences of our childhoods. Yet, there are children all over the world who are experiencing it differently.

One thing that forever fascinates me about the human experience is how many possibilities there are for us to live this life. There are at least seven billion people currently having an experience on this planet right now, who will continue to have experiences until they breathe their last breath. One day, you will have no life left to live; but every day, new life is being created. As time continues to pass, so does human life. Time is going to pass as you continue to read this book, whether you're thinking about it or not.

I cannot change your mind or change what you will experience, but I hope that in me sharing my story, you will see how you have the power to change the way you perceive your life. There was a time when I was not sure if I could forgive my dad for how he behaved in those situations, but then I thought about why he may have responded the way he did. I thought deeper about where his reaction stemmed from. In recent years, I have had to do that with myself as well. How does reflecting on my past inform my future? How do those reflections make me feel? If I were to have kids, could I unintentionally pass these harmful cycles down to them? How does one actually break a harmful cycle? I think that is a crucial part of being self-aware: taking a close look at why you are the way you are, along with what and who has led you to this moment. I can only speak about my experience, and I know that my parents were raised differently than I was. I respect that their experience was different, but that doesn't invalidate my own. I am tired of staying silent about many things that have happened in my life, and at this point, I frankly am not going to bend or twist myself to fit the narrative of anyone else.

My parents are proud of the daughter that they raised. *Is that the same woman who I authentically am?* There are aspects of myself that I know they may not understand, and I hesitate to share these parts of myself. I know my parents love the version of me that they know. *Would that love still be unconditional if they knew more of my story?* Every night, my family and I say, "I love you" or simply "love you" to each other before going to bed. When I was a kid, I considered this unconditional love, and maybe some would say it is. But I have also realized that can be a toxic habit if I don't genuinely feel it. It is hard because I do love my family, but I also don't like saying I love someone or something if I feel that I *need* to say it for the other person's sake.

Clearly, I need to talk a few things out with a professional. At the time I wrote this book, I had attempted to go to therapy and begin healing from these experiences; however, I wrote most of this during the COVID-19 pandemic, which caused tremendous suffering for so many people. Obtaining consistent access to a therapist didn't work with the time frame I had before moving to Germany, and it also wasn't an option financially. That being said, I do believe that therapy at any age can be helpful and transformative for so many people. And in the future, it is something that I plan on starting. Above all, processing and healing those specific wounds from my childhood was my biggest priority when becoming more self-aware.

Questions to Contemplate:

1. **Was there a specific experience that I feel ended the "innocence" of my childhood? Describe it.**

2. **What are my thoughts on "discipline"? Are they based on reason or internalized resentment? Explain.**
3. **What is something that I don't want to keep to myself or stay quiet about anymore?**

CHAPTER FOUR

Walking into Mrs. B.'s classroom, I approach her desk to ask, "When is the meeting for the Speech team? I have a friend who would like to join."

"The meeting is tomorrow after school. Have you ever thought about joining the Speech team, Bjerke?" asks Mrs. B.

"I don't know, not really. I get nervous talking in front of people."

"Well, that sounds like a good reason to give it a try. Why don't you come to the meeting with your friend, and we'll see if it's something you might like?"

"Okay, I'll think about it," I say as I turn to walk to my desk.

***

Middle school is such a weird time in our lives. Seriously, how awkward? I think back to when I was in 7th and 8th grade. Within those two years, I really came out of my shell. I was naturally a quiet person, and definitely a rule follower. I had some amazing teachers during those two years, who created a space in their classrooms where I felt safe to open up and express myself more as an individual. Mrs. B. was one of those teachers that changed my life. I had her as a teacher for both 7th and 8th grade Language Arts. At the time, I don't think I realized how important of a mentor she was for me, but after having her as a teacher for two years, and then as a coach, she was someone that I trusted. I felt like I could openly express my thoughts and ideas around her. I often reflect and think about that moment in 8th grade when she encouraged me to try Speech.

I went to that meeting after school, not knowing what to expect. The friend that I had made the inquiry for was one of my closest friends at the time. We had known each other since probably second or third grade, and to this day, she is still a good friend of mine. When I attended that meeting, she also encouraged me to join the Speech team along with her. There were a few other people there that I knew and were mutual friends with, so I decided to join the team. That decision was single-handedly the best decision I could've made for my personal growth and healing.

The Speech team was an after-school activity/club where each person created or curated a speaking piece that they then memorized, characterized, and eventually performed. Each weekend, on Saturdays, we would go to different schools to compete. There were several categories of speeches such as Poetry, Prose, Humorous, Informative, Great Speeches, Duo, Creative Expression, etc. When I joined the Speech team in 8th grade, I started in the Poetry category. I don't know why that one stood out to me, but I didn't question it. My gut said Poetry, so I went with Poetry.

I memorized and recited a couple poems by Robert Frost, because he was one of the only famous poets that I knew at the time. Honestly, looking back on it, it was so cringey. I was not the best speaker in the room by the judges' standards, but that didn't really matter to me that first year. I did Speech because I loved that it allowed me to speak and express myself in a new way, without having to talk about myself or be too personally vulnerable. Some would say that simply talking in front of a room of people is too vulnerable for them, and I totally get that—the fear of public speaking is a very real and common one—but it felt different to me. I was nervous, of course, but it felt so natural to be up there once I started. I also enjoyed it because whenever I gave my speech, I felt like people were truly listening to me, which was a different feeling than what I experienced in my day-to-day life.

I continued doing Speech every year until I graduated. By my senior year, I was one of the co-captains of the team and almost made it to the state tournament a couple times. In the years after 8th grade, my speeches focused more on current, relevant social issues and relatable content for people my age. Some of the topics included bullying and teenage suicide, loss of a parent or relative to cancer, and societal standards for women and girls. Sounds (sounds kind of depressing, I know, but that was what did well in the Poetry category; everyone loved a good cry and hard-hitting emotional rollercoaster.) Later in this chapter, I will talk more about the significance of one speech in particular.

***

One key point I want to make in this chapter is in regard to the significance of Mrs. B. and the transformative role that teachers can play in a child's life. I know not everyone has had a wonderful experience with a teacher, and unfortunately, some can unfortunately be quite negative. Now that I myself am a teacher and have gone through a teacher preparation program, student teaching, other practicum experiences, and certification, I fully understand how important it is for a teacher to connect with their students on a human level.

In my opinion, the most important aspect of being a teacher is establishing genuine relationships with their students. Kids especially do not want to learn from people that they do not know, trust, or relate to. Oftentimes, kids will ask, "Why do I need to learn this?" which is a completely valid question, but they ask it because they don't see the importance or relevance of it to their lives. Personally, I didn't see the importance of learning the skill of public speaking until many years later. It was because of the relationship I had with a teacher that helped me learn and apply these skills. Creating a classroom environment where every student is welcomed, seen, heard, acknowledged, appreciated, and encouraged to be curious and authentically themselves is crucial. I whole-heartedly believe that teachers being able to establish that classroom environment is one of the only saving graces of our education system today.

Unfortunately, there are so many issues and areas for improvement within the education system in the United States that cause so many challenges for teachers and school administrators. At this point, our education system is failing our society. It needs not only reform, but honestly, a radical shift in the purpose and intention behind it as well as the outside systems that greatly impact it. I understand that this is a problem that cannot be fixed by complaining or simply talking about it because it requires significant and collaborative action on a national scale. For now, and in this book, I want to focus on the aspects of it that I can control as an individual, and that is directly working in the classroom with the kids.

Knowing how transformative those years in middle school were for me, I understand how important it is for me to be intentional about what I do as a teacher. When I graduated college, I got my teaching license to teach grades K-12, but my focus was on students in secondary school (typically grades 6-12). It's cool to teach kids at that age, because they all have such strong personalities and are experiencing a lot of changes as they start to discover and explore their identities.

Learning and hearing about people's stories is something that has always fascinated me because of how different and complex the human experience is for each person that I meet. My friends and I enjoyed people-watching, so we would sometimes play this game at dinner in college where we would look around the room, pick a random person, and make up a life story for them. We took these stories seriously, don't get it twisted. Thinking of minute details like what position they played on their youth t-ball team, what their guilty pleasures were, what the biggest "real world" problem was that they faced, we came up with all sorts of random details. But the thing is, the seemingly "insignificant" details about a person are what make their perspective unique.

So often, we interact with and see people online or on TV, and we make judgment calls based on our implicit biases, preferences, and opinions (my friends and I were no exception when we played that game). Based on literally everything about us and everything that has happened to us in our lives, we perceive the world differently. People are so complex, and it is impossible to know everything about a person or what they've been through simply by looking at them. That was the point of the game: see the essence and complexity of someone's humanity while understanding that we truly don't know anything about them. It all came down to being aware of how our judgments and preconceived ideas about a person are usually wrong or completely inaccurate. Making judgments and having opinions is part of the human experience but learning to understand how they impact the way we perceive a person, including ourselves, is important when becoming self-aware. Understanding that other people will view you differently based on their own implicit biases, preferences, and opinions is one step in realizing that their perception is not your experience. We are who we are, and it is what it is, but sometimes your perception of that is flawed. That is why it is so important to listen when other people tell you their stories and to give a voice to stories that go unheard or silenced.

When I quit making art, I felt that my voice had been silenced. But because of that one teacher encouraging me to try something out of my comfort zone, I learned how to find my voice again. Along the way, my ego asked, "Why do you care so much about other people's stories? Do you even care about your own? Does your voice matter? Do you think anyone wants to hear what you have to say?" These questions poisoned my mind, but they were placed there by someone else. If you experience anxiety or have perfectionist tendencies, you may be able to relate to this idea of never being able to stop thinking or working hard to meet the expectations of someone else. I developed these tendencies and thought patterns as a child, but I wasn't aware of how much they impacted me. When I started Speech, I didn't know what I wanted to use my voice for and living with undiagnosed anxiety for many years made me face several challenges and insecurities. However, finding my voice again in middle school was a catalyst that allowed me to start breaking a cycle of generational trauma within my family.

***

The moral battle of living with how my parents "parented," and what they thought was "discipline" was, became unbearable in my early high school years.

One night, my sister was having a tantrum and my dad lost it like he usually did, and I could not let it happen again. I ran after my sister into my parents' room as my dad chased after us. There I stood between him and her. I remember quivering, looking into my dad's eyes as I said, "Stop. I am not scared of you." My dad huffed and puffed, backed down, turned, and walked away back into the living room. *How did that make him feel? What was he thinking? Was he mad at me, my sister, or himself? Would his response change in the future?*

At that moment, I was totally scared. I didn't know what would happen. I was afraid that my dad would hit me for talking back or yell at me for telling him how to "parent." In that moment, the courage to use my voice, which that I had been practicing for years in Speech, helped me use it to protect my sister. It was in that moment, that a cycle of trauma would finally end. A cycle that had been occurring generation after generation, from my parents to my grandparents and their parents before them. From that moment forward, I made it clear that that form of "discipline" was not acceptable.

These are hard memories for me to share, and we all have memories like these with varying degrees and circumstances. The only way to fully process and heal from them is to feel and have a conversation about them, whether that be with a therapist, or the person involved. However, I don't know many people who would start a conversation about their childhood with their parents with the question, "Hey, remember the time you beat me to tears, when all I wanted was your attention and validation?" These are hard conversations to have, especially with your parents. That being said, I feel that whether or not I am able to have a conversation with my parents about my childhood, it is important for me to open up a conversation about acknowledging their role in it.

For a long time, I was angry with them. But after sitting in that anger for a while, I realized that what I felt wasn't anger, it was grief. Grief for the loss of my childhood, grief for the loss of hope, grief for the loss of the idea that my parents knew what was best for me. Our parents are by no means perfect, and as you get older, you realize that they are just trying the best they can. For so many adults today, they live with undiagnosed and unhealed trauma from their own childhood. *Do they realize how much it actually impacts their life and the lives of their children? Have they ever thought deeply about this before?* This isn't necessarily their fault, because they grew up in a time when people didn't talk about this kind of stuff, but that doesn't excuse their behavior. When I came to this realization, it became a little bit easier for me to forgive them and give them the same grace that I had to give myself for letting it happen for so long. I am not responsible for their healing, but I am responsible for my own. If you don't take the time to think about your childhood and the events that occurred, you may miss out on understanding why you are the way you are today, and that will impact every aspect of your life.

I was a child when this all happened, and it wasn't my responsibility to be a parental figure for my sisters, but at times, that was the role I unconsciously stepped into. I now understand how that changed the way I experienced my childhood, as well as how it still affected me when I entered adulthood. But I want to make it clear, I am not ashamed of my parents. I am not ashamed of my actions or a lack thereof when I didn't know any better. Today, I am proud of that girl who stood up for herself and her little sister, who had the courage to voice her belief regardless of who it may offend. And I don't think I would've been able to do that, if I hadn't found my voice in Speech.

***

When I was a junior, I particularly resonated with my speech that year. It was a poetry piece about a young girl who was tired of all the standards that women and girls are supposed to live up to. She struggled to see her own beauty and strength, because she'd never had a strong example of it from her mother or in the media that constantly surrounded her.

In a way, I related to the message at the core of this piece, and I think that was noticeably clear in how I performed it. At my high school, we had something called the Variety Show each year, where kids could perform their talents, do a dance, sing a song, etc. I walked into school one day, heard about auditions on the morning announcements, and something inside of me made me sign up to audition. I walked into the choir room after school, gave my speech, and the next thing I knew, I was in.

When the night of the Variety Show came, I felt nervous, but everything felt right. When I was introduced, I remember walking onto the stage and looking out into the full crowd. This is one of those situations where being almost legally blind comes in handy, because I could not see anyone out in the crowd, (especially with the bright lights). I stood on that stage, and I poured my heart and soul into giving that speech. The entire time, I felt the words flowing out of me so naturally. I could *feel* that people were listening, that they were resonating with the message I was conveying. At one point, I was so consumed with the emotions of the room, that my words staggered in my mind, and I was thrown off for a second. I used that moment to insert a dramatic pause and continued speaking. When I finished the last words, there was a moment of silence. I think that people were trying to process what they had heard and the emotions of how it made them feel. For most people in the audience, especially other students, no one really expected something like this from me, because I had always been "the quiet girl." But after a moment's pause, a roar of applause and people standing followed. I walked off that stage feeling so proud for pushing myself to do something I had once been so afraid to do.

The next day, I overheard a girl in the hallway telling her friend about how emotional my speech made her. She definitely didn't realize that I was walking right behind her at first, because when we reached the end of the hallway, they turned to walk around the corner when she noticed me behind her. She immediately asked if that was me who gave the speech, and when I said yes, she thanked me for having the courage to stand up in front of so many people and said that my words were very impactful for her. I was so touched in that moment, because I could see in her glossy eyes just how much hearing that speech affected her, and I will never forget her genuine kindness as she unknowingly told her friend about it. The words of that speech were later used by my college professor in one of her education classes about gender roles and as an example of the role society plays in developing a child's identity from an early age. It warms my heart to know that the piece I had curated in 11th grade is still having an impact on so many people to this day, even if I am no longer the one presenting it.

***

Find your passions. I don't mean to imply that there is a limit or a certain number of "passions" that you have to find because, honestly, we all have so many things that pique our interest; we just have to find them first. So, find what makes you happy and brings you joy. When you think of something before bed or immediately when you wake up, when you hear something in a conversation or see something on your phone, something that sparks joy inside of you, curiosity even, follow that. Explore that. I think that it's important to acknowledge the little things that make us excited, because sometimes that little flutter is telling us more than we realize at first. This is especially true when it comes to seeing things on social media, whether it be a positive or negative spark to our passion.

Over the course of the next couple decades, and as technology exponentially advances, it will be crucial for us to voice our opinions about social and political issues. It is important to be aware and informed of what is going on in our society, but when you are aware and informed about injustice and destruction, there is a sense of shame in ignoring it. That being said, we live in a time where we have access to events occurring throughout the entire world with the swipe of a finger. This was not possible throughout the majority of human existence. Therefore, while it is important to be aware and informed of current events in the world at large, it is even more important to stay grounded and be active in your local community, because that is where you can truly make a visible difference. We may be able to connect to almost all corners of the globe with the flick of a finger, but access doesn't equal actualization when it comes to creating change.

Questions to Contemplate:

1. **When was the last time I was proud of myself? Why?**
2. **What could my parents have done differently when raising me? Is it difficult for me to answer this question? Why?**
3. **Write a letter to my younger self. How have I changed since I was a child? What have I learned? What do I wish I would've known at that age?**

II

ANSWERING THE CALL

CHAPTER FIVE

As an introverted person, I kept my feelings to myself as a kid, especially when it came to liking someone. I had seen how my friends were teased about liking a boy as early as elementary school, and I did not like the feeling of when other people teased me for liking someone. It made me feel embarrassed because I didn't think the other person would like me back. I was afraid of that humiliating rejection and feeling like I wasn't "good enough."

In high school, there were boys that came and went; and to be honest, none of them were incredibly special experiences. One situation in particular that comes to mind is from when I was in 10th grade. It started with a guy I knew from my school messaging me through Facebook and then eventually Snapchat. He was a couple years older than me, and one thing led to another. It started with us talking about each of our days and casual flirting, but it eventually led to us exchanging *pictures* with one another. I don't know why I initially went along with it, but I later realized that talking with this boy, making him happy, made me feel important and gave me a sense of validation. I later found out that he had a girlfriend at another school, and I felt so disappointed in and ashamed of myself, because I realized that I was not someone he truly cared about. I also would never want another girl feeling bad about herself because of the misogynistic behaviors of a shitty boy. I could imagine the pain she may feel if she found out her boyfriend wasn't being loyal or honest with her. *What did he think about me? Did he actually care about her? Why would he think that this is okay? Does he not think that this is wrong?* I felt so dirty and insecure after finding this out, because it was the first time I genuinely felt manipulated and used.

There were a few other situations I was in after this one that taught me that your curiosity cannot be quelled with superficial validation, especially if it is coming from another person. I was curious about boys, and wanted to learn more, but I would now tell my younger self, "If making another person 'happy' makes you question your worth, you are hurting yourself more than they ever could."

There was a feeling of degradation that came from these experiences, because looking back on them, I felt that I was not seen as an equal to the other person. They weren't bad people, but some of them definitely did things that hurt me psychologically and emotionally. I have learned that there is definitely a difference between caring *for* and caring *about* someone. Sometimes people can say that they care and go to great lengths to put up a facade that they care, but in the end, actions speak louder than words; ultimately, their actions proved to me that they did not understand how to care *for* someone by communicating and making sure their needs were being met.

***

CHAPTER FIVE

There is a lot of pressure in our hetero-normative society for girls to date and seek the validation of boys in middle and high school. Many of my experiences taught me some painful lessons, but I think that there is something to be said about the inexplicitly "sexual" societal standards and pressure put on young people. Our society refuses to properly educate our children about sex and sexuality while also promoting and endorsing heteronormativity and misogyny; it is quite ironic. Don't even get me started on school dress codes and how they are enforced.

That being said, I do feel that in the 21st century, people are exploring their sexuality quite a bit more openly than in recent centuries. In a way, living through quarantines and lockdowns because of the pandemic gave people the space and time to reassess how they identified to the world. When I was a teenager, family members would ask about any boys in my life. At the time, I didn't think anything of it, but when I began deconstructing the heteronormative, and even homophobic, thought patterns instilled in me as a child, I realized that I was not straight. Now as an adult, my sexuality is something I am still exploring, and there is no shame in that.

***

During the pandemic, I worked at a popular liquor store with two of my friends. When I tell you I have never before experienced so much misogyny nor been and being sexualized on a daily basis as much as I did when I was working there, damn do I mean it. I kid you not, every single time I went to work, it was almost guaranteed that an old man would either look me up and down and stare at a part of my body or say some inappropriate sexual comment. We had several managers that I could have brought this up to; however, over half of them were also men, and the other few I did not know or trust, so I didn't feel comfortable bringing it up.

Sexism and misogyny impact the lives of everyone, and it doesn't always come in the form of sexualizing a person. At one point in my life, I seriously considered pursuing a career in computer science. In fact, going into college, I was originally a double-major in German and Computer Science. Eventually my plans changed, but I remember taking a website design class in high school, because I was interested in website development in relation to business and social media marketing.

I was one of three girls in a class of about 30 kids, and my teacher was a man. One day, I had finished an assignment early, and I was helping one of my classmates with an issue he was having with his coding. My teacher came over to us and asked me why I wasn't doing my work. I explained to him that I had already finished the assignment and was helping my classmate fix a problem. My teacher was shocked that I had finished so early and said, and I quote, "Wow, you're fast at coding for a girl." *For. A. Girl.* Not only was I fast, but I was also explaining how to do it to someone else. Ultimately, I did not pursue a career in computer science, but my heart goes out to all the women in that profession, because I know they face sexism every single day.

***

One of my core memories from when I was a child, took place when I was at daycare. All of us kids were downstairs sitting in a circle, playing with Legos. At one point, a kid across from me took his block and hit the kid next to him on the head. He looked at me and said, "Huh, Amanda!" implying that I had hit his neighbor. He ran to get the lady who was responsible for us, blaming me for hurting someone. *Why would he do this?* I didn't even get a minute to explain that I had not done it, no benefit of the doubt whatsoever, before I was thrown into a timeout. That moment taught me that, no matter what the truth actually is, sometimes people won't listen.

***

These experiences, among countless others, made me acutely aware of the double standards for men and women that have been allowed within our society. But I feel that the most important thing I learned was the importance of forgiving myself for not knowing any better at the time because hindsight is the only 20/20 vision I'll ever have. My relationship with myself is complicated because I can't exactly walk away from it when I make a mistake or notice a flaw. In those moments when I felt disappointed with myself or angry at how embedded sexism is within our society, I had to find a way to move forward and learn how to value my worth separate from the opinions of another person. To do this, I held space for myself to feel that anger and disappointment. Eventually, what I once felt turned into contentment and acceptance for the version of myself at that time who was doing her best despite not knowing any better.

Questions to Contemplate:

1. **Have I ever held onto a grudge? Am I still? How can/did I let it go?**
2. **When have I been disappointed with myself? With others? Why?**
3. **How can I honor and show myself respect? How can I love myself? What does this look like?**

CHAPTER SIX

Driving has always been a sensitive topic because it is more difficult for me due to because of my eye disorder. When I was diagnosed with Ocular Albinism, the doctors told my parents that it was a very real possibility that I would never be able to drive. In fact, I failed my driver's test three times. While that is embarrassing for me to say, it is the truth. I failed because I couldn't successfully parallel park, which is particularly difficult for me because of how my eye disorder impacts my depth perception. To this day, I have never, and I probably will never, parallel park anywhere unless I can pull into the spot with ease. I would rather park fifteen blocks away from my destination to avoid the anxiety parallel parking brings me.

Before taking my driver's test, my ophthalmologist had to confirm and sign a form stating that my vision is sufficient to operate a vehicle safely, but if my eyesight gets significantly worse and they decide it is no longer safe for me to drive, my license could be revoked. In fact, every two years, they have to complete a new form confirming that my vision is stable.

CHAPTER SIX

Other than the factor of my eye disorder, there are other reasons that driving causes me anxiety. When I was in elementary school, my mom, two of my sisters, and I were in a car on our way to daycare. When my mom was pulling into the driveway of the house where our daycare lady lived, we were rear-ended by another car. This house was on a busy road right at the bottom of a hill. So, if someone is coming down from the top, they are picking up speed, and do not have as much time to slow down if they don't see someone turning into that driveway. As we were turning, we were hit by a car that was two cars behind us. The person behind my mom went to pass her in the left lane, but the person behind them did not react fast enough to slow down as we were turning into the driveway, and they hit us.

We went spiraling into the ditch on the side of the road. I remember hearing my mom scream, "OH MY GOD!" as I grabbed onto my sister, Sabrina, who was sitting right next to me, to protect her. I know my mom felt guilty about the accident that day, even though it was in no way her fault. She, my sisters, and I could've been killed in that accident. One of my sisters and my mom had to go to a chiropractor for several months afterwards, because of physical injuries caused by the accident. Meanwhile, I would face psychological injuries that would set in several years later, when I was in another accident.

***

When I was a junior in high school, I was driving Sabrina to dance class, and then I was going to the high school to attend a banquet for the National Honor Society, where I was supposed to give a speech. On one of the busier roads coming into town, the car in front of me stopped abruptly to turn onto a side street. I didn't have enough time to stop or fully swerve past them, but I had enough time to think of my sister in the passenger seat. I swerved to the right as much as I could without going into the ditch, and I put my arm across her body as we braced for impact. When we crashed, only the front left side of the car had been damaged.

Cars are replaceable, but people are not; thankfully, my sister, the person in the other car, and I were not injured in this accident, but try telling that to the guilt that flooded my mind. I felt ashamed, because my little sister was in the car with me, and I was responsible for her safety. *How would she be affected by this accident? She was okay physically, but would she be okay mentally? Would she get flashbacks like I do? Did this change the way she viewed me? How could she trust me after that?* I felt like a disappointment, because this accident occurred less than two weeks after getting my license, and my parents had just gotten this car for me that they had been saving up for. Part of me felt that my eyesight, or the lack thereof, had caused it.

I don't think many people understand that disabilities can be on a spectrum with varying degrees of severity and impact. I am almost legally blind, but I am not literally blind. I explained in Chapter 1 that the way I see the world is quite different, and it is difficult for me to explain how that may look to someone else. However, the mental and emotional impact that it has had on me is even harder to describe. It's hard to describe, because to almost everyone who sees me, the only indication of my disability is the fact that my eyes move back and forth. In the past, while most people haven't necessarily treated me any differently, the way I feel about myself and my confidence has been impacted by situations involving my eye disorder.

I am an intelligent person, and I was a particularly good student in school, but not being able to see very well made me feel stupid and incompetent at times when I was younger. When I had to go to the eye doctor as a child, I didn't really enjoy going. They frequently had to dilate my eyes to do different tests. I dreaded the vision exams because my doctor would ask me what letter I saw on the board, and they wouldn't always tell me if I got it right or wrong. I learned to know if I got it correct or not based on the tone of their voice. Knowing that I got it "wrong" made me feel bad about myself, and I felt like it reflected my intelligence in a way. I know this is not true, and I knew that it wasn't something I could control—I was born this way. But even though I knew that I was a smart kid, at that age, it didn't matter what I *knew*; it mattered how I *felt*. I felt dumb. I felt frustrated. I wished for my vision to get better, but it never did.

***

When I was in high school, after taking German classes for three years, we had the opportunity to go on a three-week trip to Germany, Austria, and Switzerland over the summer. When I was on this trip, it was a couple months after my car accident with my sister. Towards the end of our trip, we were in Switzerland, and we went to a place that had alpine coasters. They were kind of like a roller coaster that used the natural decline of the mountains to build momentum in the car you sat in.

I had gone down them a couple of times, but on the last run, I was with another girl who sat in front of me. We were trying to see how fast we could go, as any risk-taking teenager would, because these coasters could build up speed very quickly. We were getting closer to the bottom, and neither one of us pushed the break until it was too late. We ended up crashing into the back of the car in front of us, which that had two other people from my class in it. My teacher was also standing on the bridge that went over the last leg of the coaster, because she was taking pictures of us as we came down. *How was this going to affect the rest of them? Would it be as traumatic as it was for me? What were they thinking after it happened?* We all had a bit of whiplash, and it definitely was a scary experience for all four of us and our teacher who witnessed it.

I remember sitting on the stairs of our hostel that night, crying with my teacher, because I felt so guilty about the whole situation. Internally, I was embarrassed and ashamed because again, I felt that it was entirely my fault because of my vision. I had worked so hard to raise and save up the money I needed for that trip, so it was disappointing to me that it ended that way. When I got back to the United States, my parents and sisters picked me up from the airport, and we went to Arby's for dinner. I told them about what had happened and paired with the car accident from a few months prior, I did not want to drive for a while. Little did I know that when we arrived home, there would be a car sitting in the garage that they had bought while I was gone with a sign on it that said, "Welcome Home, Amanda."

***

To this day, I still experience undiagnosed PTSD from those three experiences. Any time I am in the passenger seat of a car and the driver gets a little too close to the one in front of us, or if they slam on the brakes and the person behind us gets a little too close, I immediately start having flashbacks to those memories. I no longer see what is going on in front of me. I am transported back to when I was a little kid, in the back of the car as my mom was driving, or when I was seventeen in the car with my sister. The irony is, I genuinely enjoy riding in the passenger seat and going fast in cars when other people are the ones driving. However, when I'm driving, I'm overly cautious, not only because of the potential physical threat, but also because of the emotional and mental spiral it can send me into. Driving is one source of anxiety for me, especially if there is another person in the car with me. If another person is behind the wheel, it is manageable. It is safer to have someone drive who has better vision than me, so I will usually ask someone else to drive before I offer.

Because of these experiences, I became very aware of the weight guilt carries, and it's fucking heavy. A beautiful part of my healing has come from understanding that your secrets keep you sick. I don't need to hide in shame about not passing my driver's test right away, and it took me years to release that. I've also realized that sometimes, there are secrets you are carrying that are not even yours. From my own experience, I carried them with me because I am an empathetic person, but that doesn't mean they belong to me. Empathetic people often develop this skill through experiencing and internalizing the pain of other people, whether or not those other people caused the pain or expressed it to them. I learned this at an early age from several of the experiences I shared in previous chapters, but I didn't realize until recently that it wasn't necessarily a "skill" but a coping mechanism.

Talking about difficult memories from when I was a kid and dealing with other forms of trauma in my childhood have allowed me to give those internalized secrets back to the people they belong to. I am able to express and be vulnerable about how those situations impacted me, because I no longer have any internalized shame about what happened.

So, if you are holding on to any guilt, please let that be where you focus your attention, if you know there are situations in your past that you need to heal from. At the end of the day, I understand that I cannot change my actions. I cannot control the actions of others or change what happened. Even with reliving and having flashbacks to those moments, I am learning from those experiences. Life really can just disappear like that. In that split second of the crash, my life could have been extremely different if it still existed at all.

***

These are stories that I probably wouldn't have shared if I hadn't taken the time to reflect on the answers to the questions included at the end of this chapter. I hope that one of the most important things you take away from this book is reflecting on what you have already experienced. You already have the knowledge and capability to grow inside of you. The reflections you have while contemplating your answers to the questions at the end of each chapter are what allow you to become more self-aware. In releasing my shame and guilt for the "accidents" I've been in, I've learned that the bigger the mistake, the more important the lesson, and the harder it is to learn from.

Questions to Contemplate:

1. **What events in my past do I still blame myself for? Could I control the circumstances at the time?**
2. **What secrets am I holding onto that I'm scared to admit? Are they my secrets to keep?**
3. **What do I think about when I can't fall asleep? Do I find myself ever overthinking or analyzing something I said or did? What triggers these thoughts?**

CHAPTER SEVEN

"*Hör gut zu!*" says Frau E. over our class trying to get our attention as chatter fades out.

"Frau, this is too much work," says a kid to my right.

"I don't get this. Why do I need to know this?" says another in front of me.

"Life is tough, I know. But we can do tough things. We have one more page *und dann, sind wir fertig!*" cheers Frau E. from her podium at the front of the room as we near the end of our class. "You are getting 10 college credits out of this. 10! That could save you quite a bit of money if you decide to go to college," she continues as a couple of students grumble to my left about still not wanting to do it.

"You all have made it this far learning a new language. Learning a language is tough but being able to communicate with more people around the world, especially coming from the US, is something to be proud of. I am proud of all of you for making it this far," she says.

Frau E. has been one of the most influential people in my

life. On the same level as Mrs. B., she is someone who is truly enthusiastic about not only educating students in terms of achieving academic success but educating her students on what it means to be a good, kind person to yourself and others. She was my teacher for all but one semester of my German classes in high school. I will describe in Chapter 17 how she has still played a role in my life as a colleague and mentor. Apart from many other teachers that I had, you could feel that she cared. She genuinely roots for her students as if they were her own kids. Unfortunately, there are bad apples in the public school system, but she was always a light in a world of darkness for so many kids.

***

In the United States, a kid's junior and senior year begin to be consumed with thoughts of the future and what one will do after graduation. I began taking classes in high school for college credit when I was a junior. At my school, we called these College in School (CIS) classes. Some examples of the classes I took were chemistry, public speaking, and German. We also had Advanced Placement (AP) classes that I took as well. I decided to take them for a couple several reasons. As a bright kid, one of those reasons was that I needed to be challenged. Another was that that my teachers told me it would be a good idea, because I may be able to save money by already having credits going into college. Therefore, this could reduce the number of classes I would have to take to get my degree at the university.

Were they wrong? No, not necessarily. At the time, I believed that this was the best decision for me; and honestly, I do not regret taking any of the classes I did, because they did provide me with a challenge. I was also able to complete my degree and certification to teach two subjects in four years, which probably would not have been possible without having those credits. There is no shame in taking longer than four years to complete a Bachelor's degree, but college is so expensive in the US that many students cannot afford it and don't even consider it as an option. Since graduating and knowing that only a couple of the college classes that I took in high school actually helped me after the final exam, I get a weird feeling in my stomach whenever I hear teachers and schools talk about college classes using the same language as a business deal. There is a lot of pressure on kids to believe that they "need" them, but that is not always the case.

I'm sure there are people who took that German class and never spoke the language again, but I also know a considerable number of us who did go on to pursue a degree or career where we use our language skills. The point I'm trying to make in this chapter is not to debate about the relevance of the classes themselves, but to compare the practicality and genuine application of the skills and knowledge acquired within those classes to the pressure and stress that came along with them.

I know I've heard teachers and adults say that college is not the only option, but in my experience, it feels like it's the only option they prepare us for (and even that's a stretch). There were career days and booths at lunch, but the atmosphere of this conversation was filled with the underlying tones of expectation and a sense of judgment. Most high school students feel pressured to have the "correct" answer to the question, "What are you doing after high school?"

One of the biggest concerns of my generation is the gross amount of debt many of us take on in order to pay for higher education. The cost to attend even a public university in the

United States is astronomically overpriced and an obvious sign of where the true value is being placed: profit, rather than education. Universities are institutions that are focused on collecting a profit and guaranteeing that that profit continues to increase each year by continuing to raise tuition prices and applicant outreach. I would argue that the institutional goal of most universities in this country is not to provide their students with a phenomenal education for the sake of *education*, but for the sake of attracting new candidates to exploit.

Due to the increasing prices of tuition, there is a pressure put on young teens to do what they can to save as much as they can, if going to college is something they see for themselves in the future. This often leads to students overwhelming themselves with three, four, five, in some cases even six college classes, while managing their coursework for their high school classes. Some students, similar to in my own case, need more of a challenge that the public school cannot always provide in the mainstream classroom. However, I feel there is a line between a healthy challenge and overworking yourself, which was hard for me to recognize.

As a teacher, I have seen many students who are constantly stressed trying to manage their course load but are not usually successful in managing that stress. Stress, working hard, and thinking about your future are all normal aspects of life in our society; but if our students are not also being taught how to manage this stress and we continue placing crushing amounts of pressure onto their shoulders to attend college, this only leads to burn-out and the potential for them to develop further mental illness and instability.

***

I've heard people say that touring college campuses is like

buying a home or buying a wedding dress—you just know when it's right because of how it feels, and it's also similarly super expensive. When I toured the campus of the university I ended up attending, it felt like a place I could see myself calling home. It was the first school I visited, and after seeing other campuses, nothing matched the feelings I had when I toured there. People say to trust your intuition. Listen to the whispers of your soul. That is how I felt being at that campus and seeing how everything was laid out. It also helped that there was a lot of nature surrounding both campuses, and it had a similar small-town vibe that I was used to. This not only made me feel safe, but it also made a college education feel accessible to me. With my vision difficulties, I had spent the majority of my educational career up until that point sitting in the front of the classroom, and I had to usually rely on myself to take good notes and advocate when I had difficulties. I knew that a smaller school would be the best option for me. Several of my teachers in high school had also gone to that school and shared stories from their experiences there that got me interested in the first place.

After completing my undergraduate degree, I am thankful to have received the education and connections that I did. However, do I believe that I got my money's worth? Well, that's a whole other question that requires some tiptoeing and walking a fine line along gratitude and constructive criticism. Of course, there are things that could have been better, and the institution has work to do to catch up with the times. But in the end, I am grateful to have had the opportunity to continue my education in the first place.

***

My point is people will probably tell you that you have to

get into a good school in order to get a respectable job, and that you shouldn't follow specific dreams. Most of the time, if someone tells you that you can't do something, that is usually them projecting their insecurities onto you. They may believe that that they cannot do it themselves, and their limiting beliefs are trying to limit you as well. I hope to never work a job that I cannot tolerate, a job that makes me feel unpleasant inside and not fulfilled. I've done it before, and I understand that for many others, it's the only option available to them at the time. I am learning that sometimes being happy requires you to prioritize your fulfillment over immediate stability, and that being able to do so is a privilege.

When I began traveling and observing diverse ways of life, I realized how little I know about the world. I've noticed that in Europe, there is a unique perspective on "working" and "work culture." Beyond labeling yourself as "what you do," my eyes have been opened to new possibilities for creating a fulfilling life. Unfortunately, I feel that our current school system does not adequately prepare students to be global citizens who are considerate of complex histories and differences between societies. One thing I wish we could normalize in this country is taking a gap year or time away from school to explore ourselves and learn through experience.

I find it interesting how we put juniors and seniors in high school into the mindset that they *need* college, or they *need* a specific job, or they *need* to join the military because they have to do *something*. As you grow up, you are learning about what interests you and what you enjoy. We shouldn't have to make these decisions to do certain things because we *have to* in order to "survive" in this society. With the advancement of artificial intelligence and the reach of social media, I believe that collectively, new generations of people will likely decide not to work in one job or even career field for their entire lives.

When you become aware of your own capability to create the life that you desire, you learn that that you don't need to follow a specific outline, you can design your own. Building up your self-awareness takes time and doesn't come right away. Think about how you make friends. You spend time together, and you get to know them over time. so Similarly, it will take time for you to get to know yourself in this way as well. The bright side of this is that you are stuck with yourself for as long as you live. You've got plenty of time to figure it out, while meeting some cool people along the way. But don't take that time for granted, because it's never guaranteed in the same way that the people in your life now are not guaranteed to be there in the future. And when you step into that power of creating the life of your dreams, you will begin to realize that it was the life you were always meant to live.

One of the many life lessons that I will take away from my time in Frau E.'s classroom is simply: Be a Good Person. She would tell us this if she noticed any behavior issues in class and as we left her classroom at the end of the hour. This one simple phrase has been a life motto for me and countless other students of hers, I am sure, because that is one brick in the foundation of a happy life. Happiness and being kind are not exactly skills you can learn from a lesson in school; but like I did, there are many things that you can learn simply in the way you interact with others.

I now see that if you have poor relationships with other people, including yourself, you will find it difficult to live a happy life. While I believe education is important, if you can't read or do math, you are still able to live a happy life. The relationships you have with people are what determine your impact on them. You hear of people who were bullied in school, and then they grow up and have successful careers where their school bullies come back around asking for a job or advice. They realize that the kid they bullied in school maybe wasn't so bad after all, and now has something that they need or want. I think this can apply to fake friends, but it also applies to being a bully to yourself.

Relationships are key. There are people in your life, whether you are in high school, college, working as an employee, or being an employer, who will go on to do amazing things in their lives. Especially when you are in high school, it is easy to get caught up in cliques and this idea that this time right now is everything. This is totally normal because you haven't really experienced a world outside of that mindset. But while you are in high school, it is important to always be kind, because you never know how life will play out when you walk out those doors on the last day. Some people you won't ever see again, and others may circle back into your life. People don't always remember what you said to them, but they remember how you made them feel. They remember the impact you had on their lives if it was a substantial one. Regardless of if it had a positive or negative impact, people remember.

***

Something else that I would like to talk about is the guilt that I felt, and occasionally still feel, about attending such an expensive university. It was a private college that opened the door to many amazing, privileged opportunities and connections for me. Before I even graduated high school, I knew I would be the one responsible for paying for my higher education. My family did not have a lot of money growing up, and my parents have been living paycheck to paycheck for as long as I can remember. This stress was unconsciously placed on me as a child and has led to me needing to dismantle my own financial insecurities as a young adult. A child should not have to worry about their parents' finances, but this happens to a lot of children, especially if they are the oldest in the family. My parents tried their best to provide my sisters with everything we needed, and I am grateful for all that they did with picking up multiple jobs, but I now understand that their money was never any of my business.

That laid the foundation for my future, and now that I am financially able to take care of myself for the most part, whenever I am able to travel or find a cool opportunity, there is an underlying sense of guilt. My parents have access to seeing my primary bank accounts; and once I began teaching, the amounts within them slowly grew larger. I know I have nothing to be ashamed of, and I am proud that I have been able to put habits in place so that I am responsible with my money. However, I know that there are other people out there who sometimes feel ashamed of having more money than their parents.

My parents have been supportive of me following my dreams. Even if there is uncertainty with the outcome, they are proud of me for having the courage to do so. That leaves me with this last point to end the chapter: you can have the support of your parents, grandparents, friends, teachers, community, etc., but the most important person who needs to believe in your dreams is *you*. Sometimes this requires you to take a risk which can be scary and daunting when the majority of your life so far has been planned out. But on the other side of a risk is usually one of three things: a reward, a lesson, or a new opportunity. If you do not believe your dreams are possible to achieve, then why should anyone else?

Questions to Contemplate:

1. **What sparks my curiosity? What am I interested in learning more about?**
2. **What brings me joy? What does happiness feel or look like to me?**
3. **What is something I wish I learned sooner? What is something I wish we learned more about in school?**

CHAPTER EIGHT

"What are you most excited about for this new chapter?" asks my mom from the driver's seat.

"The parties!" jokes my dad.

"Or the boys," says one sister.

"She's kidding, Dad," I say. "I think I'm most excited to be on my own and start fresh, meet new people."

"I'm an adult," says another sister mockingly next to me.

This a phrase I jokingly said to my mom on my eighteenth birthday; and ever since, I have said it when I make an *adult* decision or do something on my own.

I suck the air through my teeth and respond, "I'm excited to do things on my own, but I don't know about all the adulting stuff."

As we arrive at my college campus to move me in for the first time, the colorful trees and pillars at the entrance welcome us in. My mom pulls up to the curb as my dad rolls down the window. We are directed where to park and unload. Two girls meet us with a large cart, and they begin unpacking the tightly packed truck my family had spent so much time and energy moving around. And, just like that, everything was out of the truck and being carried to my dorm.

There are apartment-style buildings surrounding an open courtyard. We walk through the main entrance, and find the bookstore, mailboxes, security, commons area, and front desk. We lug my stuff to the right, where I scan my ID for the very first time, and as we walk down the hall, we pass the bathroom on the left and the lounge on the right. We then reach the second door on the right side of the hallway—Room B13.

***

Moving your kids to college could honestly be a competitive sport, because I have never seen a more meticulously packed vehicle than when my family moved me into college. My parents, three younger sisters, myself, and my entire life packed up into boxes made the hour and a half commute to my new home for the next four years.

After finding my room, my family helped me unpack all of my stuff because I read somewhere that you should let your family help out—they will be having a tough time adjusting to your absence at home as well. My mom was unpacking my bedding, and she saw that I had brought my pink baby blanket with me to school, and she immediately started crying. My mom is an emotional person, and she can cry at the drop of a hat. We tease her for it, but the truth is, I can be the same way, except I have pushed down many of those emotions or expressed them in different ways in the past. I am the oldest child in my family, so I knew it was going to be hard for my parents, especially my mom, to say Goodbye. I ended up arriving before my roommate, so I tried to unpack and organize as much as I could so it would be out of the way when she arrived. There wasn't a whole lot of space in the room to begin with. I knew college dorm rooms were going to be small, but wow, they really pack you in there like sardines.

For people who decide to go to college after high school, this may be the first time in your life that you've spent an extended period of time away from your family and the life you grew up with. Oftentimes, going to college means leaving the safety and security of home; but I suppose that's the point. Your entire world changes.

In this time, you realize that you become responsible for yourself in the ways your parents and teachers were responsible for you as a child. You have to essentially learn how to parent yourself—in all aspects of the term. You'll have to learn about doing laundry, cooking food, saving money, processing emotions, and making other important life decisions. I also learned in this time that the world and adulthood is not what I expected. At the same time, I don't know what my expectations were in the first place.

One of the most difficult parts of moving to college was learning how to live on my own, surrounded by other people who are also learning to live on their own. I feel like every first-year student in college feels at some point that they are alone and that everyone else has it all figured out. Even though they told us in orientation that it that was a normal feeling to have, it wasn't something we ever continued to talk about. It was almost like that understanding disappeared after the second week of school. The fear of missing out, or FOMO, is a real thing, especially when you are trying to make new friends.

***

On one of the very first days during orientation, the RA (resident assistant) on my floor took us outside onto this open grassy area to play a few games to get to know the people living in our hallway. We played a game called Birdie on a Perch, where we each had to find a partner that wasn't our roommate. Our RA played music and when the music stopped, you had to run and find your partner. One person had to be the birdie and sit on the bent knee of the other person, who had to be the perch.

I looked around at all the girls as they started pairing up. I made eye contact with a girl who was a little taller than me and had brown hair.

"Wanna be partners?" she said.

"Sure. My name is Amanda."

"Hi, I'm Jade. Nice to meet you."

Little did I know that that one simple get-to-know-you game would introduce me to a lifelong friend who has taught me that your friends truly are the family that you choose. I could go on and on about how phenomenal of a human she is, because she has been there with me through so many challenging times. She has never judged me and has truly redefined what "friendship" means to me.

***

While I made a lifelong friend on one of the first nights of college, building friendships when you initially move in is not an easy thing. I remember sitting in my dorm room feeling so alone because I hadn't felt like I hadn't made a strong connection with many people. When you leave home, regardless of if you go to college, get a job, join the military, etc. you realize that the friends you had when you were younger may not have actually been good friends or people you genuinely resonate with. Yes, you got along well and shared some good memories, but chances are, many of those friendships were circumstantial. That is okay. I have learned

CHAPTER EIGHT

that life brings in the people you need exactly when you need them.

The thing is, there is a lot of peer pressure that goes on when you move to college, because you feel like everyone has it all figured out and that they're making friends so easily. People definitely go with the crowd, even if they are trying to give the impression that they aren't, and I could see through that bullshit right away during orientation.

Here's where I noticed that my eye disorder started impacting my ability to make friends. There were times when I would be walking to class, and I would see someone that I knew either from class, my orientation group, or someone that I had met somewhere along the way. Because I cannot see far distances very clearly, I would usually recognize this person right as they were walking past me, and it was a little too late to say hello. This can come off rude to people because they will wave at me from a distance, but I am not able to see it, so they think that I ignored them. I know this because one of my friends told me one time that, before they knew more about my eye disorder, they thought that I was ignoring them whenever they would wave at me from wherever they saw me. When they told me this, it explained why so many people from my orientation group and people that I had met the first year had stopped saying hi to me. It honestly hurt my feelings, because this is not something I can control, and I had expressed that I had an eye disorder that made it difficult for me to see.

I can explain to people until I am blue in the face that I am visually impaired, but because they do not see what I see, they do not understand what I mean, and they ultimately forget that I have a disability in the first place. This made it difficult for me to maintain connections with people at the beginning of college. However, it is a good detector for me of people's character and their genuine interest in a friendship with me. I learned that even if I do communicate with people that I have a disability, sometimes, they won't remember and may need to be reminded in the future.

***

For many college students, you have to live in a dorm with at least one other roommate, which teaches you about cohabiting with another human being. When I was accepted into and had made my decision of where I would go to college, I joined a Facebook page that had all of the incoming first-year students in it. This was a place where people posted questions and introductions to get to know the campus and our class better before arriving in the fall. Many people, including myself, used this as a way to find a roommate.

At first, my roommate and I got along really well. We were both in Speech in high school, and we even went to each other's graduation parties. During the first couple weeks of living together, everything was going well. But eventually, things started going south.

I honestly have a challenging time sharing my space with people, because as an introvert, when I need to recharge, I need to be alone. My roommate was also introverted, which ultimately meant she would frequently be in our room as well. *How did she feel while we were living together? Were there ever any issues she didn't know how to bring up?* I think what it comes down to is that we did not communicate our spatial needs very well, and it created other issues within that relationship. I think that is the hard part about moving to college and rooming with someone you don't know very well. I have three younger sisters, so I grew up living and sharing a room with another person, but it is quite different when you barely know someone at first. Usually, the dorm room you are sharing is probably not very big. You are in a stage of your life where you are on your own, and not only are you learning about how you function best in that small space, but you are also semi-responsible to the other person you are living with to communicate those needs. However, if you don't know what those needs are, it is difficult to communicate them.

To make a long story short, by Thanksgiving Break, we had decided that it was better for us to go our separate ways, and she moved in with another girl down the hall. *How did this decision make her feel? Could things have been worked out if we had tried to start fresh? How could I be a better roommate in the future?* I learned a lot about living with another person during those first few months, but I also learned more about myself. For me personally, I began to recognize coping mechanisms, toxic behaviors, and unhealthy habits when I looked at how I was raised and how I was continuing to live my life.

After reflecting on the final conversation I had with her and our RA, I realized that I interrupted her when she tried to twist my words or actions. I learned that interrupting people is an internalized traumatic response to feeling like I've been misunderstood or that I haven't been heard. When I was younger, if I did have something to say, I was taught that I had to interject my point if I wanted it to be heard. People did not always expect me to say anything, or they would cut me off when I did start talking. This was a pattern that I had not seen before, and once I saw it, I noticed that many of my other family members did this too in conversations. It has taken practice, but I am now more intentional about listening to others. I value communication, and I want to hear what they are saying, to understand their message, and not to just respond to it immediately.

That is one example of something I learned about myself from living with my first roommate, but there have been other things that I have learned from living with other people since then. These habits and behaviors are not always easy to notice, let alone change or improve. I'd even say that the hardest part is recognizing these patterns in yourself, but. But once you recognize them, that is where the true work starts. For some, they begin this work unconsciously as they learn how to live on their own or with other people. And for others, they start to connect the dots and take active control in dismantling those habits. It started off as the former for me, but by the end of my undergraduate career, I had been taking an active role in unlearning and relearning how to live harmoniously with myself and other people.

In Chapters 9 and 10, I will talk about when I lived in Salzburg, Austria for four months, during my sophomore year of college, but something similar happened with my roommate while I was studying abroad. I'll admit, I have learned that I am not always the easiest person to live with. I am independent, and I need my space to recharge. If I feel that I cannot let my guard down around a person, I don't feel comfortable in their presence, and it makes me frustrated. This was the case with both of these roommates in particular. I did not know them very well; and therefore, never felt truly comfortable around them. At times, I did not trust them either.

I felt bad that our roommate relationship ended poorly, because I think that I actually had quite a bit in common with both of those girls, but unfortunately, things didn't work out. I sometimes regret how I handled both of those situations, but they were lessons in communication. This is something that I will have to continue working on as I live with other people. Even though I have had positive roommate situations since then, I have learned how important it is for me to feel comfortable in the other person's presence. If I feel judged or the potential to be judged, I know that it will not work out. I immediately put my guard up, and once it's up, it's rare that it comes down—something else I'm still working on.

***

Whether it be a tough situation with a roommate, or a falling out with a friend, losing people in your early adulthood is completely normal and part of the process as you change and identify yourself as an adult. I have maintained some amazing friendships from high school that have lasted over ten years now, but learning how to communicate and work through that physical distance after high school was a challenge. It really shows you who your genuine friends are, and it makes the relationships even stronger. Some friendships may have been genuine in high school, but it is totally normal for people to go their separate ways after graduation. To those people who I'm no longer connected with, I still wish you peace and love for a happy and fulfilling life.

I think that the friendships you create when you initially leave high school can be superficial, and again, circumstantial. That isn't necessarily a bad thing. This time period in your life, regardless of if you went to college or not, is extremely transformative because you are changing so much and remembering who you are and who you want to be in this world. Naturally, the friendships you form may either come and go, or adapt and evolve.

Speaking from experience, heartbreaks from losing a friend

are the hardest thing to go through in my opinion. Whether it is in middle school, high school, or any time in your life really, letting go of people you once considered your world is a challenging thing to do. At the end of high school, I lost a friend as well. Looking back, it was over something so petty, and I had hoped we could work it out. We ended up attending the same college, and after seeing them grow and mature over those four years, I am so proud to have known them and had the opportunity to call them a friend at one point of my life. I believe that our falling out gave us room to grow as individuals, and I truly do wish them the best.

Losing friends is a natural part of life, whether you outgrow the friendship entirely or you grow apart in different directions. I've also learned that sometimes, that people are there simply for character development. It is okay for me to wish them well and let them go, because I may be the main character in my story, but that doesn't mean I'm the main character in theirs.

I will share more about my international travels in later chapters. During, but during those months when I studied abroad, I learned more about myself and also that I don't know a lot about the rest of the world. When I came home, there were some people that I no longer felt connected with. I'll admit, pushing people away and ghosting them wasn't the best solution (and don't you worry, I'll get my karma for that one in Chapters 11 and 13). For a while I tried to cope. Eventually, those coping mechanisms didn't work, and the people I was surrounding myself with no longer resonated with my frequency or who I wanted to be. At the time, I said that I outgrew the friendship, but specifically, I didn't connect with these people in the same way anymore. Regardless of how the situation panned out, there was a time where I did mourn the loss of those friendships that once meant the world to me.

We had some good times: filling a friend's room with balloons to surprise them when they woke up, decorating Jade's door at midnight for her birthday while she shouted at us from the other side to go to bed, spending countless homework sessions in the lounge on the Aurora B floor, almost starting a fire because of a popcorn maker, getting free pizza from our friend who worked at the pizza place in town, and the list goes on of memories that I will forever cherish. But unfortunately, I no longer resonated with some of those people, and I had to let them go.

You learn so much about yourself during the four to five years after graduating high school, that when you look back at each year individually, it can feel almost like looking at a different person each time. I think back to the thoughts, ideas, and opinions I had when I was younger. When I was away from my hometown for those four years I spent at college, I had time to realign my perspective and form my own identity. However, in the beginning of my college journey, it wasn't always easy. I grew up in a small rural town, and I hate to be a buzzkill, but racism is basically bred into the majority of kids who grow up there. For those of us who make it out and see the perspectives of people who grew up very differently than us, we learn that there are things one has to unlearn. I will specifically touch on this in Chapter 15.

When you are living on your own or with other people, you begin to examine the unique habits and mannerisms of how you live and what your needs are. How do I need to be taken care of? What makes me feel happy? What makes me feel safe?

What creates consistency and stability in my life? How do I communicate my needs with those around me? The truth of the matter is, I understand why so many adults pressure young people into following the path paved by those before you—it is easy, and it provides a sense of consistent stability. I believe that psychologically, we as human beings need to feel some sense of stability or consistency in our lives to feel comfort, and that looks differently for everyone.

When I graduated college, that was something that continued to ring true for me. If you go to college, you can find stability in your class schedule and daily routine, and if you don't go to college, you find it in other ways, such as the consistency of a job. Regardless, there comes a point when you no longer have that consistent schedule or goal to be working towards like you did in high school, and you have to confront the reality of being an adult. The possibilities for what you can do with your life are endless. That is both empowering and overwhelming at the same time. It is also not something you are really prepared for.

Overall, going to college was the most transformative experience I've had so far. If I could tell my 18-year-old self anything before she even stepped foot on that campus, it would be this:

You are going to change more than you ever thought possible over the next four years. You will be tested by your courses the curve balls of life. You will meet some amazing human beings who will redefine family and friendship for you, but you will also lose some along the way. You will have high highs and low lows. You will travel to beautiful places in the outside world, but you will also uncover some of the darkest shadows inside your mind. You may not recognize yourself when it's over, but trust in the process and your intuition that guides you. You are not alone.

Questions to Contemplate:

1. **What makes me feel safe? What creates consistency and stability in my life?**
2. **How can I improve the way I communicate with others about my needs or emotions?**
3. **How do I welcome or resist change?**

III

SHEDDING LAYERS

9

CHAPTER NINE

Before I had made my college decision, I remember going to an open house for my university near the Twin Cities. At this open house, there were different tables for each department such as Education, Environmental Studies, Accounting, Global Business, etc. where people described their experiences and the opportunities that they had had throughout their time there. One theme that stuck out to me was hearing stories about having the opportunity to study outside of the United States for a semester. It was a program you could do to travel and gain experience at an international university, while also receiving credit towards completing your degree in the US.

This was something that I was interested in, because I wanted to continue studying German in college, but I also wanted to gain some experience being in the same place with people who spoke it as their first language. So naturally, I kept this in my mind throughout my first year. About half-way through the year, I received an email about an informational meeting for those who were generally interested in studying abroad. At this meeting, they talked about the different programs available, the cost comparison of studying in each country, how the credits would be transferred, etc. Most students at my college typically studied abroad during their junior year, so when I attended this meeting, I had done so to be proactive. I hadn't yet made up my mind whether I would apply during my sophomore or junior year.

One thing I did know for certain is that I wanted to study in a country that spoke German. At this point, I had studied the language for four years in high school, and I had declared it as my major. Because I took CIS German in high school, I already had quite a few credits completed for my German degree. I decided to go a year earlier than most people typically do, because I felt that in order for my language skills to progress, I needed to be immersed in the language as soon as possible. After comparing the programs in Germany and Austria, I decided that the program in Salzburg, Austria would be the best fit for me.

As I was going through the application process, it felt so natural and like I was simply following the motions of what I knew needed to be done. I completed the interview, the preliminary meetings, visa appointments, etc., and before I knew it, I was going to be living in Austria for four months during the start of my sophomore year.

Before we left in the fall, everyone in our program had to attend three orientation meetings to go over some logistics and begin getting to know each other. When I attended those first few meetings, I could tell everyone was trying to read the room and make a good impression. Being raised to be the "quiet" girl and needing to be aware of my surroundings at all times because of my eye disorder led to me also being an extremely observant person. When I am having conversations with people or I overhear others talking, I pick up on slight differences in tone and changes in behavior, which I have now learned is also a trauma response for me. Nonetheless, I think back to my initial impressions of the people on my program. While most of them were pretty accurate, it is interesting to look back on those first few meetings now, knowing how much we have changed since then. At the time, I didn't realize how impactful those relationships would be.

Before we arrived in Austria, I was not sure if I would connect with very many of them, especially because I was the youngest person and I didn't really know anyone beforehand. Honestly, I was prepared to be a lone wolf if I needed to. However, I am incredibly grateful to say that I found my people, and that was one of the biggest lessons I learned throughout college: it may take time, but you will always find your people. At the end of the day, I had some form of a relationship with everyone. It felt like we were together basically 24/7, so it's kind of hard not to. In total, there were about twenty-eight people in our program that were from my university. We also had a professor from our university, and his wife, in charge of our group and leading the trip. We got along because we basically had to; our time there would've been miserable if we didn't. But honestly though, what I love the most about them is that we made the best of our situation and the most of our time there. We didn't have to be friends, but most of us chose to be. Not only did I establish connections with the people on my program, but I also met several other people from around the United States, Germany, and Austria. But regardless of how strong those relationships felt in the moment, most of them were situational friendships; and I don't think there's anything wrong with that. Some of the relationships I made with people were genuine, and they have become some of my favorite people on the planet.

I had to work a lot of long shifts over the summer beforehand to save up money to be able to afford this experience on my own, but it was all worth it. This was one of the most memorable times of my life for which I am eternally grateful for, and it truly was a once-in-a-lifetime experience that I worked so hard to financially make happen.

***

While living there, I learned so many lessons—some were definitely harder than others. I will share a few of those difficult lessons in more depth in the next chapter; but first, I would like to share some of my favorite memories from those four months of my life.

I personally enjoyed getting to experience cultural events firsthand, because I had been learning about them for four years in school. We were only there for four months, so we were able to experience many of the fall and winter events, such as the Krampuslauf and the Christmas markets. We also definitely put our own little spin on a few of them as well, literally. One of our assignments for a class we had with the professor from our university was to create an event that centered around a cultural aspect of the community and country we were in. One guy in our group really enjoyed swing-dancing, so he decided he was going to teach us all how to do various kinds of swing-dance that we could then do when we went to Oktoberfest in Munich, Germany the following weekend.

Oktoberfest is something else, y'all, and if you don't really know much about Germany or German culture, Oktoberfest is probably the one thing you do know. It is important to note that Oktoberfest is more of a Bavarian tradition than a German one, but it has become the common stereotype that most people associate with German culture. Because of that, most people on my program wanted to go. Most of them didn't speak any German or have any prior experience learning about German history or culture,) so it was an easy way for them to be exposed to it.

The small group that I went with spent the ride to Munich drinking on the train and pregaming, because Oktoberfest is basically the equivalent of a glorified State Fair both in the activities there and the prices, so beer was going to be expensive. Don't get me wrong though, we each had quite a few beers while we were there as well. As we would go from tent to tent, many of us would couple up and swing dance in the streets to the music that was playing from each tent as that we walked by. If I'm being honest, there are several parts of that day that I do not remember very clearly.

One memory that I will never forget is when my group and I were waiting for the train to take us back to Salzburg. One of my friends and I began dancing and spinning each other around in the train station, just having an absolute ball. This older woman, who was also clearly a tourist like us, was laughing along as she took pictures and videos of us dancing. We were wearing our Lederhosen and Dirndls, so she probably thought it was the perfect "German" photo-op, but I'm sure we also looked absolutely ridiculous. Overall, 10/10 experience that I will forever cherish.

***

As far as classes go, we had an environmental class with the professor from our university, and we also had classes such as Art History and Philosophy with professors from the University of Salzburg. Our Art History professor was one of the most fabulous women I have ever met in terms of style and the way she carried herself. Honestly, I am convinced she works for the Austrian government in some way, because she was able to get us into so many private and restricted parts of museums and historic buildings anywhere we went with her.

Our Philosophy professor was a bit of a character, and you could tell he wasn't exactly the biggest fan of ours, (which at times was understandable, because we probably were annoying at times). For example, I remember one day in class, a guy went out into the hallway to buy a bottle of juice from the vending machine that which was right outside the door of our classroom. He didn't bother to shut the door or anything behind him, and this particular vending machine made a loud whirring sound every time it moved. So, as my professor was trying to lecture, you could hear this machine squeaking in the background, and the rest of us still in class could not hold in our giggles. When the guy came back in the room, he was oblivious to the fact that we had all heard him in the hall. He looked at the professor who had stopped talking, and said, "What?" with a confused look on his face, and we all burst out laughing. Our professor cracked a little bit of a smile before an angry face swept over, and he started ripping him a new one. After that day, we were not allowed to leave the classroom from the minute class started until the very end when he dismissed us.

***

Even though the main focus of us being in Austria was to study and gain experiential knowledge, we were also encouraged to travel if the opportunity presented itself. Over the course of those four months, I traveled to eight European countries and several cities within Austria. In particular, London, England was a place that I had dreamt of visiting since I was a little kid. I was obsessed with learning about British history, so when I had the opportunity to visit London over Thanksgiving, I was in heaven. It was the perfect time to visit, and keeping in theme with the holiday, I took a bit of time to express the gratitude I had for the life that I was living and the people who had made it possible.

I also went to Split, Croatia on a spontaneous trip with a friend from my program for a weekend, and that was also a trip that I am so grateful to have had. I remember we went to a club there one night, and we had absolutely no idea what any of the lyrics were in the music, so we just kept singing the lyrics to *Despacitio* during the chorus of each song as we danced the night away. It is memories and experiences like those that I will always remember as highlights of my young adult years.

During that time, one thing that made it so special was how we were able to explore several aspects of ourselves that we may not have had the space to explore back in the US. It is one thing to learn how to live on your own in a country you are familiar with, but when you are on your own and in a foreign country, you really learn a lot. Because you are living in a country with a bit of a different lifestyle, you discover things that interest you and bring you joy that may not have been obvious or possible in your home country. There is a bit of duality in that as well, when you start to uncover some of the darker parts you've maybe never seen.

Like I mentioned, our main priority while we were there was to study, hence why it is called "study" abroad. But honestly, after the end of class each day, that first word basically disappeared. We went out to the bars in Salzburg pretty regularly. Don't get it twisted, we did not always go out to get drunk. The bars and Biergartens were a place to meet and socialize with other younger people. The Augustiener is a perfect example of this. Many of the times we went there, we went there for one beer and to play cribbage. In fact, that was my "cultural event" for the assignment in the class with our university professor. I held a cribbage tournament where each person had a partner, and our whole group sat in one of the Staals at the Biergarten, played cribbage, and drank casually.

Student Night and Karaoke Night were some of our favorites at the local bars, because beers were only two Euros each, and the vibes there were always good. We also didn't have class on Fridays, which was nice when Karaoke Night was on a Thursday (that way people weren't always showing up to class super hungover). Some of my favorite conversations with people occurred during our 30- minute walk home from the bars, alongside the river that ran through the middle of the city.

From the Eristoff ICE war to the guys' wine chugging contests, experimenting with alcohol was something we all took part in, especially because it was legal for us all to do so in Austria, whereas, in the United States, most of us weren't of legal age yet. Drinking culture is quite different in Austria and Germany as well. I know the stories I share paint a picture that looks one way, but I can promise you, most of us weren't out binging every weekend. For some, that was their choice, and I'm sure they learned a lot, but for most of us, it was a way to experiment. "Experimenting" would be a theme of the trip, I would say.

CHAPTER NINE

Not only did I experiment and test my limits with alcohol, but I also experimented with drugs as well, because why the hell not, you gotta live a little. Since studying abroad, one phrase that I live by is, "If you're going to do irresponsible things, you do them responsibly." It was something I wanted to experience, so I made sure to do it in a safe manner. I trusted the people I was with, and they trusted me. While in Amsterdam, I babysat people on shrooms, we smoked in the street and drank coffee at a cafe, and overall used it as a tool for self-exploration and to further enjoy the life we were living on a more intense level. It is important for me to share that it was not always butterflies and rainbows, and that is a natural effect of experimenting with anything. There were times when I smoked a little too much weed and got a little too high to the point where I didn't know if I was gonna come back down from it. What I learned from those experiences is how important it is to surround yourself with people you trust and who actually care about you, but also that you have to listen to your body and allow it to do what it needs to do. Moderation is also a good thing.

***

Finally, I want to talk about something that I heard many people say while living abroad, and I have heard many people say since. Let me present an example: a group of people from our program go out to the bars and get a little too drunk. One person starts to wander the streets on their own and does not want to be followed or walk back with the group. They are obviously very drunk and don't know where they are going. Another person says, "Leave them be. They're an *adult*. They'll learn from the consequences." Another example situation: Two people meet at the bar and have several drinks together.

They leave the bar to go back to someone's place, and their friends say, "Well, they're *adults*," but you feel in your gut that something is off.

I think that many of those situations where people used the phrase, "They're an adult," similar to the examples I just gave, could have been potentially dangerous and avoided. I understand why people said what they did and that ultimately, you will have to learn and face some sort of consequence for your actions. But there were several times I questioned if I should have done something different in those moments, because even though we were all legal adults, that does not mean we were making the best decisions for ourselves. I have learned through those experiences that you truly need time on your own as an "adult" to make those dumb mistakes. I could sit here and tell you that it's okay to have no fucking clue what you're doing sometimes, and that's part of becoming an adult, but that's not always helpful if you're placing yourself in an unsafe situation. I'll rest my case here, but ultimately, I am grateful to say that we all survived our semester abroad with memories to cherish for a lifetime.

Questions to Contemplate:

1. **Describe an experience that changed my life? Why was it so impactful?**
2. **What is one moment I wish I could relive? Why? How did I feel?**
3. **What is something I wish I could experience? Do I think I ever will? Why?**

CHAPTER TEN

NOTE: This chapter describes an event of attempted suicide and the prevalence of mental health issues.

In October of my sophomore year while studying abroad, we had a ten-day break. Many people on my program decided to travel during this time. A group of my friends and I wanted to go to Paris and Amsterdam. One of them had a French exchange student from Paris stay with him when he was in high school. He was somewhat still in contact with him, so we ended up staying with his family while we were there for a couple of days.

We, of course, went to a couple of the typical tourist locations, but I think my favorite was the Louvre. When you are there, you have to see the *Mona Lisa*. I mean, I suppose you don't *have* to, but like, why wouldn't you? I must admit, it is remarkably interesting to walk down that wing of the museum where the painting is on display. You walk down this one hallway with hundreds of masterpieces and then into a room filled with even more masterpieces, but you know the majority of people are all there to see one painting. There were hundreds of people crowding around one little glass case, trying to get a picture. For me personally, because my eye disorder significantly impacts my vision, it is difficult for me to see things that are farther away. I had to get to the front of the crowd in order to get a decent glimpse. Let's just say that if you want to get to the front, Minnesota Nice definitely isn't going to cut it. Even once you make it there, you're still standing at least six or seven feet away from it, so the clearest view I was able to get was a zoomed in picture on my phone. The painting is smaller than many would probably imagine, but it was still very cool to see, nonetheless. Honestly, it is a little overhyped, in my opinion, considering how many other masterpieces and beautiful pieces of artwork there are in that museum, but it is a legendary painting and worth the visit regardless.

My friends and I got to see a local perspective of the city from the friend we were staying with. His mom cooked us some authentic French food, which was so bomb, and his dad let us sample some of his brandy that he had been making for years. I don't know what exactly this guy's relationship with his parents was like, but damn did they put some trust in him, because over the weekend, they left to go on a little vacation. They told him that he could have a party while they were gone and left him money for alcohol, food, and other goodies. Whew, let me tell you, that was a party!

Paris is a beautiful city, but I think that in order for you to get the full magical effect, it is all about who you go with. It is called the City of Love for a reason, and I hope to go back there one day with a significant other. Definitely don't get me wrong though, my friends and I had a wonderful time in that city, but it wasn't all fun and games.

On one of our first days there, we stopped at an ATM, and I pulled out about 200 Eros, which was most of what I had left in my bank account at the time for travel. After going to the ATM, we got on the train to go to our next destination. This was a pretty crowded train, and we were standing almost chest to chest with the other people there. I had just been to the ATM, so I made sure to hold onto the money in my pocket so that I knew no one could steal it—hello foreshadowing.

At one of the stops, a man had to get by me in order to get off the train. He put his arm around my waist to move me to the side, and when I pulled my hand out of my pocket to push his arm off of me (because like, we don't need to be grabbing women that way), I knew immediately what had happened. He sprinted off the train, and I couldn't bother going after him. He had stolen the 200 Euros from my pocket. I didn't say anything to my friends about it, because I was so pissed that a man had not only made me feel that uncomfortable, but he succeeded in his mission too. It was so fucking frustrating. I was embarrassed, because I knew I should have put the money into my wallet right away, but I didn't. Now, I wasn't sure how I was going to pay for anything over the course of our trip. Let me remind you, we were going to Paris and Amsterdam, and we were still in Paris.

Thankfully, my parents were able to deposit a little bit of money into my account, so I could pay for things like an AirBnB, food, etc. until I got back to Salzburg where the rest of my money was. I remember stressing out the entire time we were on this trip, because I was constantly thinking about money and worrying if I'd have enough to pay for a meal. Many of my friends on this trip came from wealthier families than I did. One girl was even able to have her mom wire her $2,000 while we were in Paris, simply because she asked for it to go shopping, which only made me feel even shittier.

To this day, I don't think any of them knew what was going on in my head throughout that trip or even what had actually happened. I keep a lot of things to myself, especially when I feel that others will judge, torment, or ridicule me for them. Before writing this, I thought I had fully processed and came to terms with those feelings from that time period in my life. But it wasn't until after writing it out and editing it that I fully came to terms with it. I would hope that those people would not have treated me differently if I would've told them the truth, but a part of me does wonder sometimes how things may have been different. They were some of my good friends on the program, but we had only known each other for a few short months.

I remember sitting in our AirBnB in Amsterdam, having an anxiety attack because I was so stressed about my finances. This story really highlights financial insecurity that many people experience if they did not grow up with a lot of money in the family. While most of the cost of this program was included in our semester tuition, I had to work overtime the summer before and apply for another student loan in order to be able to finance it. I am incredibly grateful that my parents were able to help me out occasionally after that incident, so eternally grateful, because I know that money was also super tight for them. I will talk more in depth about these feelings of financial insecurity in Chapter 17, because it is something that a lot of young adults experience.

The last thing I want to say about that trip to Paris and specifically Amsterdam is this: do you know how frustrating

CHAPTER TEN

it is to be in some of the coolest cities in the world and not be able to fully enjoy them? I know how much of a privilege it was to even be there in the first place, but that didn't make going through those struggles or that anxiety any less stressful. It was definitely a learning experience, but alas, there were way worse things that happened while I studied abroad.

***

Traveling to Paris and Amsterdam, along with several other European countries, sounds like the most amazing dream; and it honestly was a surreal experience to live through that I didn't think was possible for me when I was a child. However, with those high moments, there also comes the lows—we love balance.

During my time abroad, I was falling out with a friend, Allan. Our friendship was very toxic, and the excuse of studying abroad forced me to take the time and space I needed to let that fizzle out. Except, it wasn't as smooth as I had thought it would be. We had an argument one day about communication and wanting to talk things through (which is difficult when you have a seven- hour time difference). Nothing anyone said crossed any lines or anything, but we were both frustrated and upset with each other. I didn't have anything else left to say, but apparently, he hadn't said everything he needed to.

A couple of days later, my study abroad group all went out to the bars to celebrate going on a weekend hiking trip in the Alps the next day. We were out at Karaoke Night, and I got a call from my friend on Snapchat. I debated answering right away, considering how our last conversation had gone, but reluctantly, I answered the call. When I answered, I didn't hear my friend's voice; it was his sister. She told me that my friend was in the hospital. He overdosed on pain pills.

The feeling I had in my stomach when she told me that... Well, there was no feeling, I suppose. I felt like my entire soul had left my body. I couldn't believe what I was hearing. It didn't feel real. Memories of a time in high school when a girl I knew, who had taken her own life, came flooding back into my mind. What if the same thing was happening now to him? I don't know if I could live with myself if it were.

I quickly rushed out of the bar to catch the next bus. I saw that the next one wasn't coming for a little while, so I decided to walk back home. When I turned around to start walking, I saw a group of a few guys from my program heading back, so I walked up to them. As I approached, I heard one of them say, "Should we wait for Amanda?" and a guy named Devin said, "Hell no, I'm leaving that bitch at the bar!" Devin and I frequently disagreed on many things morally and politically, so this wasn't exactly a surprise. One of the other guys looked at me and said, "Don't listen to him. He's drunk and going through some shit. Some people go through things you might not always see."

Feeling absolutely disgusted, I walked back home. Throughout those thirty minutes, my mind was racing with one question after another thinking about if my friend would be okay. *What happened? What was he feeling? How did he get to this point? Did I miss something? Were there any signs that I didn't see? Has he mentioned thinking about this before, or did he make any comments that seemed off? Was there something I could have done to help him sooner? Should I have done something differently? Why would he feel that this was the answer? What will happen if he doesn't survive? What will happen if he does?* As I mentioned, Allan and I were having a falling out at the time. We weren't nearly as close as we used to be, but I still cared about him,

CHAPTER TEN

and I hoped that he would be okay.

Later that night, I had a tough time falling asleep. When I finally dozed off, my dreams were very vivid. In one of them, I was back at the bar. I looked down at my phone and saw that my friend was calling. When I picked up the phone, I heard his voice telling me to walk outside. I quickly walked out of the front entrance, and there he was, standing in front of me in Salzburg, Austria. Then, the dream changed. I was walking down a gravel road in rural Minnesota; it was the gravel road leading up to his house. It was after dusk, and as I walked up his driveway, I noticed a glow from the fire pit in his backyard, so I walked around to the back. When I turned the corner of his garage, I saw him lying in the grass next to the fire pit. I ran over to him, calling out his name, trying to wake him up, "Allan, Allan! Wake up, Allan! Wake up! You need to open your eyes, Allan! I'm here, you're gonna be okay! Don't give up yet! I'm gonna call for help! Please don't give up yet! Open your eyes!" And then, I woke up.

The next morning, I climbed a mountain, both literally and metaphorically. Our study abroad group was spending that weekend in a little cabin on the top of a mountain. We spent most of the first day climbing and taking in the beautiful views of the Austrian Alps. (Shout out to Miley Cyrus, because she wasn't wrong when she said that it was 'all about the climb,' truly a rewarding experience.) When I reached the top, I started crying because the intensity of not knowing how Allan was became overwhelming. All of the emotions that had been going through my body and my mind throughout the last 24 hours caught up to me all at once. I knew I wouldn't be able to talk to him for the next few days, because there was no cell service on top of the mountains... Duh, we were thousands of feet above sea level, in the middle of nowhere. I broke down crying, because I couldn't stop thinking about how guilty I felt being literally on top of the world, adrenaline pumping, high on life, while my friend was lying at his rock bottom in a hospital bed, probably having his stomach pumped, not knowing if he would make it to tomorrow.

In those three days in isolation on that mountain top, my entire study abroad group became incredibly close on a human level. Climbing mountains is one of the most magical experiences, and one that I hope you have the chance to do someday. It is difficult mentally and physically going up, but it is worth it every time when you make it to the top and see the view from above. The state of peace and sense of accomplishment that you experience is unmatched. That weekend alone is why I will always have peace and love for every single one of those people that were on my trip, even Devin.

On one day in particular, it was incredibly foggy outside, and you couldn't see anything past three feet in front of you—which is so dangerous on top of a mountain. So, we stayed inside and played cards the entire day. I taught myself how to shuffle cards into a bridge, and just about all of us learned how to play cribbage. If you didn't know how to play cribbage after that hiking trip, you probably weren't ever going to learn, because when I say we played cards for at least ten hours that day, that is not an exaggeration. Granted, as the hours passed and the beer started flowing, nothing was really making sense after a certain point. We hadn't even drunk that much, but alcohol has a greater effect on the body the higher in elevation you are.

Because we were completely isolated up there, I took some

time to be by myself, journal, and begin to process my thoughts and emotions. I desperately wanted to hear Allan's voice and to know that he would be alright, but that wasn't a possibility at the time. I had some close friends up there that I talked with and told them about what had happened. Regardless of the falling out, I wanted to support Allan as best as I could over the next few weeks. My friends were supportive in thinking of ways that I could do that while also giving him the space he needed, which helped me not to feel so powerless. My religious beliefs, which I will describe more in Chapter 12, evolved a great deal during that time. In my belief, heaven and hell can be states of consciousness that we experience on Earth. Both are always present in our world—exhibit A, the difference in experience between me and my friend.

At the end of that weekend, we hiked back down the mountain. I low key lost my shit on Devin when I slipped going down a muddy hill, rightfully so, because he made a snide comment about me needing to be more careful. I was not having it after the way he spoke to me the other night, walking home from the bar.

At the bottom of the mountain, I was able to check my phone before dinner to see that Allan would eventually be okay after spending a few days in the hospital. When we all got back on the bus to go home from our trip, I filled everyone in about what had happened, and I thanked everyone for being supportive, whether they knew they were being kind or not. In those moments on that mountain top, those people unconsciously helped me get through some dark and scary emotions, but those emotions were nothing in comparison to what Allan must've been feeling when he attempted to take his own life. It really gives a person perspective.

While the friendship between Allan and I eventually did end, this experience reminded me how important it is to tell people you care about them when they mean a lot to you, even if the relationship itself isn't exactly the strongest. You never know when they won't be there anymore.

***

Death as a concept and as a metaphor is something that I frequently think about. Not to sound morbid, but I have also contemplated what the world would be like without me in it. I don't think there is any way for me to write that without sounding suicidal, but I promise that is not how I mean it to come off. However, suicide is an important topic to open a conversation about, especially with how serious and prevalent mental health issues are in our society.

What has this world become? How did we get to this place where so many people struggle with their mental health? Has this always been something prevalent within humanity? Did humans in the past just not have the awareness or vocabulary to describe it, or is this something that has come with our evolution and societal collapse? Why are there so many people desperately looking to escape this world? How did we create a world that so many people want to escape? These are some of the questions that my mind circles back to when thinking about mental illness and its prevalence in American society.

There is so much beauty to experience in this life on our planet, but so many people are not able to see that, because they're caught up in their own darkness. This isn't their fault by any means; how do you escape the darkness when you're never taught how to? Is it something that one can even truly escape from? What we're commonly *taught* to do is take medication and pretend like everything's okay. There is no shame in taking medication, and there isn't anything inherently wrong with it; in fact, it can be life changing for some. However, we need to have this conversation about why that seems to be the default and if there's something else that we're missing. I don't know what the best way to go about the mental health crisis is, but I do know that something needs to change on a societal level.

It is okay to not be okay, and I truly mean that. Not that type of bullshit where people say it, but what they really mean is, "It's okay to not be okay… but only when it's convenient for others." No, I truly mean that there is no shame in acknowledging that you are not okay right now. I'm not going to tell you at this moment that everything will be okay, because there are times where that genuinely doesn't help. When it comes to struggling with mental illness, healing from trauma, escaping abusive situations, coping with eating disorders or self-harm, etc. I feel that it can be more damaging to try and convince someone that it is "going to be okay" or that "things will get better."

Many of us have been conditioned to believe that where we are right now is permanent, but it isn't, it truly is not. The feelings you have in the present moment can be very intense, and so it is easy for us to beat ourselves up about where we're at and how we are doing right *now*. But the present moment is fleeting and constantly changing. Where you are now is not where you are going to be forever. So, if everything really isn't okay at this stage of your life, that is okay. As human beings, we are changing so much more than we often realize with each day, month, and year that passes. The person I am today is not the same version of me that I was a couple months ago, but during that time, I wasn't always aware of the minor changes that were occurring. Subtle changes in the way I think, the way

I feel about myself, and how I identify to the world around me are occurring, as I continue to live and experience new things. Where you are now, is not where you will be in the future.

For me personally, I have struggled in the past with anxiety. Overthinking and getting stuck in my head were common occurrences that I would look down on myself for, which only made me spiral into more thinking. What I have learned is that I shouldn't blame myself for having to deal with those things, as many other people deal with them as well.

I know that it can be hard to scroll through social media and see the curated picture-perfect lives that people present online. But just because you are being exposed to their highlight reel does not mean that they are not also struggling. Posting about and discussing the struggles we face is extremely vulnerable, and quite frankly, I don't think anyone is obligated to expose themselves to the unfortunate negativity and hate that comes with being vulnerable on social media. We all deal with the effects of mental illness to different degrees. Don't get me wrong, it definitely sucks when you can't get out of your head or out of your bed, but you are not going to be there forever. It is okay to struggle, and it is okay to not be okay. You are not alone. So please, be kind to yourself, and be kind to others, because at the end of the day, we're all just trying to make it through to the next.

Questions to Contemplate:

1. **What makes me feel alive?**
2. **How am I feeling right now? Am I comfortable with talking about my emotions? How can I express my emotions rather than suppress them?**

3. **What has someone said or done to me that tore me into pieces? How did I put myself back together?**

CHAPTER ELEVEN

NOTE: This chapter describes an event of sexual assault and the topic within societal discourse.

As I mentioned, studying abroad was one of the best decisions I made, but it also opened the door to a hallway full of more doors that I didn't think I'd ever have to open. I don't think any woman thinks she'll be sexually assaulted one day, but unfortunately, it happens to a majority of women. When many women talk about their stories and make commentary on the misogynistic behaviors of men, many respond with, "Well, it's not *all* men." To that I say, it may not be *all men* who treat women that way, but the fact that damn near *all women* experience some form of sexual abuse in their lifetime, means that this is an issue involving *all people*, because women are not the only ones affected.

I attended an open lecture led by a professor in the Gender Studies Department at a local university (not the one I was attending), and they asked anyone in the room who, as long as they felt comfortable sharing, has experienced, or knows someone who has experienced sexual violence in any way to stand up. Almost the entire room stood, both men and women. They then instructed those of us standing to sit if we reported the incident and the person was held accountable for their actions. A handful of people sat, but the majority of us stayed standing. There were about 200 people in this room. The professor went on to make the point that this demonstration perfectly depicts why so many women, men, and non-binary people do not report the abuse they've experienced, because in our society, we generally do not hold sexual offenders accountable for their vile actions.

This is why I share my story today. I hesitate to go into detail, because if you have experienced sexual assault or any form of sexual violence or aggression, it can be traumatic to read someone else's experience. It can make you relive your own trauma. So, this is your heads up, if you'd like to skip this portion of the chapter.

***

One night, a group of my friends from one of the other US programs and I went out to the dance clubs. A couple of them wanted to drink, but there were also a few of us, myself included, who weren't drinking that night and were the DSFs (designated sober friends, as we called it, kind of like DD for designated driver). We were hopping around from dance club to dance club, until we ended up at our final destination. We had been at this last club for about 45 minutes, when one of my friends needed to go to the bathroom.

If you've ever been around a group of girls when one of them has to go to the bathroom, you'd know that they rarely ever go alone. So, I walked with my friend to the bathroom, and she took care of her business. As she washed her hands, she looked at me, and her face began to look very pale. Before she had a moment to say anything, she ran back into the stall and started throwing up in the toilet. I followed behind her to hold her hair back and get her some toilet paper to wipe her face when she was done. After she finished throwing up, she told me to wait outside of the bathroom for her while she collected herself—in true puke and rally fashion. I walked out the door to wait for her outside the bathroom, the biggest regret of my entire life.

I had been standing outside the door for no more than three minutes when a man approached me. He said something to me in a language that was not German or English, so I did not understand him and gave him a confused look. He grabbed my hand and pulled me around the corner. The bathrooms at this dance club were in a hallway towards the back of the club. At the end of the hall, there was a slight corner that turned towards another little hallway that led to an emergency exit. The second we turned that corner, he pushed me up against the wall and began sliding his hands all over my body and under my clothes as he shoved his tongue down my throat.

What happened next, I am deciding to keep private for my own safety and peace of mind, but in a few words, I was sexually assaulted. Frankly, I do not think that I should need to describe any more details of my assault for you to believe that I was, in fact, assaulted.

I don't know how long it lasted, but I was eventually able to push him off of me. I ran back to my friends and told them that I needed to leave. I didn't say anything to them about what had just happened, but thankfully a couple others said they wanted to leave as well, so they came with me. I am so grateful that they did because I did not feel safe being by myself. I was

CHAPTER ELEVEN

quiet the whole way home.

When we finally got back to our apartments, one of the girls pulled me aside and asked if I was alright, saying that I seemed a little off. I told her that I just had a headache and wasn't feeling like myself. *Did she believe me?* That night, I sobbed in the shower, trying to wash his hands off of me, but the worst part was trying to sleep. The events of what had happened earlier kept replaying in my head over and over again, until I finally cried myself to sleep.

My fight, flight, or freeze response kicked in as soon as he grabbed my hand. But in that moment, I was confused and disarmed, so I froze. As *it* was happening, something snapped in my mind, and I was able to push him off of me and flee. But a couple of nights later, I saw him again. And this time, I was ready to fight.

I was at a different club and with a group of people from my own program this time. In our group, there were about two or three other girls and about five or six guys, (Devin being one of them). We were on the dance floor having a blast, after also having many drinks, when I spotted him looking at me from across the room. I made eye contact with him, and he looked away, but out of fear, I couldn't take my eyes off of him. When he glanced back over in my direction, I stared him down. *Why was he here, looking at me? What was he thinking? Would he try to do something again?*

He started to walk over towards me and my friends, holding my glare, and as he got closer, he placed his hand on my lower back to move around us. I snapped around and pushed him backwards. He started to say something, again not in English or German, and made a lunge at me. All of the guys in our group immediately pulled me back as they jumped in front of me to push him away. One of them had a beer bottle broken over his head, but to be honest, I do not remember who actually hit him with it. A few bouncers walked over to our group and told us that we all had to leave, so we did. We were honestly all in shock with what had just happened, but especially me, because I did not expect the guys to defend me the way that they did.

As we were walking back home that night, one of the girls asked me why I had stared at and pushed him. *Should I tell her the truth?* I basically told her that he had grabbed me in places that I did not want to be grabbed and that it wasn't the first time. Getting the hint in my voice, she didn't press any further, and that was the last time it ever came up in conversation. *What did she think after that? Did she know what I was hinting at? Had she experienced anything like that before? Would she believe me if I told her the truth? Should I have been honest with her?*

Growing up, and in school, you learn shockingly little about things such as safe sex, teen pregnancy, STDs, and especially sexual assault; but when you do, you don't always think about how or if they will actually happen to you. I never in a million years thought that I would be sexually assaulted, let alone writing about it.

Living in this world as a woman or someone who is nonbinary is quite a distinct experience than living in it as a man. Before I studied abroad, I had heard from various people that as a young woman, I would need to be extra careful and aware of my surroundings when I traveled. I knew that at the time, and I understand it even more now. There will be men who do not understand what it feels like to be a woman in this world. There will be men who will not understand what it feels like to walk around fearing that, if you are not careful enough or

CHAPTER ELEVEN

make one wrong move, such as standing outside of a bathroom for a moment too long, someone will take advantage of you.

I share my story, not to get anyone's sympathy, but because I know that there are so many other people out there who have experienced this as well. Any form of assault is traumatic; and while I acknowledge that comparatively, my experience may not be as severe as others, my experience is valid.

Unfortunately, there will be people, who will read my story and not believe me, or think that I am being dramatic, or even dare to say that I deserved it. But no one, *no one*, ever deserves to be sexually assaulted. Ever. I don't know why the fuck our society still thinks that this shit is okay or even that it's "funny." Explain that to me because I don't get it. I don't understand why people blame others when they come forward. I don't understand why people accuse others of lying when they try to tell their story. Like, for real? That shit's not only embarrassing, but it is absolutely disgraceful and disgusting that we live in a society where this happens regularly. It shouldn't happen, period. I learned so much from this experience (much of which I'll describe later in this chapter). One being that I now understand why girls never go to the bathroom alone, and the second being that there is nothing scarier in this world than a man who can't handle rejection or feeling like he can't overpower a woman. And if you are offended by or thinking of ways to contradict any of this, then maybe you are a part of the problem.

To this day, I never told any of the people I was with on either occasion the details of what I had experienced or what he had done to me, because quite frankly, he would not have been held accountable. I thought it would be easier to suffer in silence. It took me a long time to fully process and recollect my memory of what had happened. The truth is the memories will never fully go away. That experience and the memory of it will affect me for the rest of my life. I've heard people say that the brain tries to forget trauma, but the body always holds onto it—what your mind forgets, the body remembers. In the weeks and months afterwards, I struggled to feel physically close to anyone.

There were other instances where I was interested in people while studying abroad, but it never went very far because my body and mind weren't ready to be that intimate with anyone. That is, until I returned home and met Evan.

***

When I came back from studying abroad, I knew I had changed. Who I was as a person and the goals I had for myself, were different than before I left. The things I valued were a little different, and the people in my life before I left no longer aligned with what I needed after coming home. Unfortunately, I had to cut those people out of my life, and I do occasionally regret the manner in which I handled things. However, I know that despite how much I knew it would hurt, it was the best decision for me. It was hard to do, and I am sorry for any hard feelings, because I wish peace and love to all involved. All I have left to say about those people is: thank you for making my first year of college one to remember. I am grateful to have experienced life with you, but our season ended sooner than any of us expected; I had to make room for a new chapter.

On the first day of the semester, a few of my friends were in Eleanor's room. We were catching up and spilling all the tea that had happened during the last semester, while I was gone. I didn't tell them the specifics of what had happened to me the previous semester in Austria, but I vaguely mentioned that

CHAPTER ELEVEN

I'd had some not so wonderful experiences with guys. As a promise to each other, Eleanor had us all put our hands on *Bad Feminist: Essays* by Roxanne Gay, and we recited the following to one another:

> *"I solemnly swear that I will take no shit, and do no harm, stay away from toxic people, and not give a shit about boys."*

Two things about that "promise." One, I wish I would have actually read *Bad Feminist: Essays* before that semester; and I admittedly didn't start reading it until after I began writing this book... Wow, would it have maybe saved me some time and energy. And two, if those words are not the epitome of foreshadowing, I don't know what is, because a couple of days later, all of that apparently went out the other ear.

Jade wanted to introduce me to a friend she had made while I was abroad, so we went over to his dorm room one day to hang out. When I met him, I was immediately attracted to him. I clearly wasn't looking to start a relationship at the time, but something about the way we clicked felt so natural. At one point, he offered me some beef jerky (not knowing I was a vegetarian), and when I turned it down, he started blushing. Jade laughed and said, "Amanda's a vegetarian, but nice try," and the way he tried to play it off was so cute. He hung out with our friend group a couple times after that, but the next weekend is when we really connected.

We were all hanging out at a few of our guy friends' apartment. A few of us decided to go for a walk and pick up some food at the dining hall. While we were walking, Evan and I kept gravitating towards one another; and when we got back to the apartment, I made my move and held his hand. We exchanged Snapchats before I left to go back to my apartment, and the rest is history. We were together almost every single day after that.

At the beginning, it was fun and innocent. When we officially started dating, I saw a lot of potential in where we were going, and from what he told me, so did he. *Was that how he really felt?* Slowly, but surely, he started to feel more distant, and the way he treated me changed. *Why had his behavior changed all of a sudden? Were we getting too close too fast? Were there any difficult relationships or breakups in his past? What was going through his head?* We'd make plans to do one thing, and he'd end up doing something else with one of his other guy friends without giving me a heads up that the plan had changed. There were times when I would be in my room most of the day, either crying or really upset, because I thought we had plans to hang out and he left me waiting or cancelled them at the last minute. When we did eventually spend time together, he didn't say anything about what had happened or why he had changed his mind. He made me feel like it was no big deal, and it made me think that maybe I was overreacting. *Why did he do this?* Ultimately, the potential I saw was no longer the boy in front of me.

In the end, when we broke up, he didn't even want to talk to me in person about it. I genuinely believe that he had a lot to work through on his own. There were so many issues he had brought up throughout our relationship from his past that I knew he still hadn't processed. I thought that I could be the person to help him through that, but inevitably, that was not possible. I had to learn that you can't always be the one to save someone else. Sometimes, you gotta know when it's time to walk away. When I went to his dorm to talk with him about the breakup, he couldn't even have a conversation with me in person, because he was worried that I would cry, and *he* didn't know how to handle the thought of that. *Why did he feel this way? Was it hard for him to talk about his emotions?* So instead, I went to the lounge on his floor, and we talked over the phone. It was more so me talking and speaking my peace while he listened (and for the record, I didn't even cry), but I felt like I got my closure after that "conversation." Afterwards, he came into the lounge, we hugged, and went our separate ways for the summer.

Even though I felt like I got some closure, my heart was still broken. I definitely would not say that I was in love by any means, but I really did care for him. He helped me start my healing process after what had happened the previous semester in Austria, but when we broke up, that healing journey took on a whole new meaning. It was also only a couple of days before my 20th birthday; and looking back, I am glad it ended when it did. Although, I definitely would not have thought that it was probably for the best at the time.

The summer after that semester is a complete blur to me, and it is basically blacked out from my memory. I blocked it out not because of alcohol or another substance, but because it was a really grim time for me, and I honestly didn't want to remember the pain. That summer, I knew I had to do a lot of healing, but I avoided it by drowning out the emotions with working at my summer job. I was not okay emotionally. I was not okay mentally. I was not okay. Especially when I started to put together the pieces of how toxic the relationship actually was, every day felt like walking through a tornado of emotions. You go through quite the range of them after a breakup.

I didn't understand why someone wouldn't want me in their

life, or how they could treat someone so shitty. *Why did he push me away? Why did he make promises we both knew he couldn't keep? How was the breakup affecting him?* I was pissed, and I honestly lost my mind at times trying to understand why he never appreciated all that I did. I was sad, because I wished he would have cared for me half as much as I cared for him. But in that pain, I had to learn that sometimes, the love you try to show someone, isn't a form of love they are capable of receiving. Sometimes, it goes right over their head, because they don't understand what it genuinely feels like, let alone be able to respect, appreciate, and reciprocate it. When I learned that, I truly understood how important finding your partner's love languages is—being. Being able to find someone who is compatible and aligns with how you express and receive love.

When it comes to how I treat other people, I now do my best to treat them the way they *ought* to be treated, because I've experienced first-hand how challenging it can be to develop self-respect, let alone self-love. If you take away anything from this section, let it be this: for the love of god, please make it your number one priority to learn how to love yourself, whatever that means and looks like to you. Our existence confuses the hell out of me, but at the end of the day, you are the only person who is stuck with you, for the rest of your life. Don't you at least want to enjoy your own company?

Questions to Contemplate:

1. **What are red flags for me in a potential partner?**
2. **What are my non-negotiables in a relationship?**
3. **When was the last time I cried? Why?**

12

CHAPTER TWELVE

I went on a trip that forever changed the way I perceived the world, religion, and my spirituality during the fall semester of my junior year. For a while, I struggled to understand and articulate what I believed in, because I have both witnessed and experienced how religion can be used as a tool to heal, but especially, as a tool to harm.

Before going on this trip with my friends, I questioned the religious beliefs with which I was raised. Afterwards, my thoughts became a little bit clearer in terms of what *my* beliefs were, apart from what I was taught growing up. I was baptized, raised, and confirmed in the Catholic faith, and at the time of my confirmation, I really did believe in it all. I enjoyed reading the Bible, and I tried to get something out of going to church (even if I felt that, at times, going to church was one of the most boring, out of touch ways to strengthen my relationship with God—it didn't always feel personal). But as I continued throughout high school and went off to college, I explored and did my own research into my religious beliefs and the history of the religion itself.

At the core of the faith, my beliefs aligned at the time with the premise of following in the ways of Jesus Christ and his teachings; however, when it came to the specifics mentioned in the Bible, I could never get over the fact that it is a book written, interpreted, and translated by human beings, over the course of many centuries. Objectively looking back at history and seeing the way it is written to favor the victor and cover up truths that do not always fit the agenda of those teaching it, why would the Bible have been any different?

I attended a private, Catholic liberal arts college, so I was not too hard-pressed finding to find old books and artifacts describing and depicting the religion or finding people to have discussions about it with—we had nuns and monks living on our campuses, for crying out loud. After doing much of my own research and taking classes about other world religions, I took note of the similarities, correlations, and overlap there are between many of them. After realizing which aspects of each aligned with what I felt to be "truth," I made my peace with the fact that I no longer supported, identified with, or practiced Catholicism.

For a while, I had to work through some internalized aggression towards people of faith, because of my experiences with many of those practicing around me when I was younger. I judged people for blindly practicing a faith without questioning it. I remember a time when I was sitting on the living room floor at home, sobbing, having a conversation with my parents about what I believed. I felt so frustrated, because they didn't seem to be able to understand what I was saying, and I couldn't understand why they, and so many others, could support a Church that has done so much evil in the name of "good." At the time, neither of us were really able to articulate what we believed in or how we felt. It was hard for me not to be judgmental of them and the Church they supported.

Now, after processing my internalized feelings and exploring my own spirituality further, my beliefs are a lot more compassionate towards those of a different faith or belief than my own. I am in a place now where I actually genuinely enjoy listening to and having discussions with people about these differences. I think religious tolerance and being open to new ideas was the most impactful lesson I learned during my time attending a Catholic institution; and ultimately, I feel that we all need something to believe in that keeps us going when life gets tough—to each their own.

On this trip with my friends, we had conversations about and experiences regarding religion and spirituality that opened my eyes to new perspectives that I had never seen before. One realization I want to share with you involved my friends and I going for a walk. We took this trip during the middle of fall, when the leaves were at their peak of changing color. Because of my eye disorder, seeing the details of each leaf is not something my eyes are usually capable of. However, during the fall, because each leaf is changing at a different rate than the one next to it, my eyes have an easier time picking up on the differences in color. I remember walking through that forest with my friends, looking up at the trees surrounding me, taking in the neon colors of every single leaf. The fall time is my favorite season of the year because of that vibrancy. As the wind blew through the trees, it looked as if the sky was on fire in the most beautiful, symbolic way. It is truly a magical time because of the metaphorical significance trees have in relation to the seasons of human life. And at the time, I felt that I was in a period of shedding layers for the sake of evolution, like the trees.

Sitting underneath the fiery canvas above us, my friends and I talked about our inner conflicts surrounding our identities and how the world perceived us as we were exploring them. We all concluded that everything we knew, we had been taught. Whether it was by a person, people, or an experience, everything we were was a product of circumstances. Our lives were created through cause and effect. What we think becomes what we say. What we say becomes what we do. What we do becomes who we are. And there we were, the layers of our egos falling away, as the leaves fell to the ground around us.

I won't claim to be wise but being aware at a youthful age can be really depressing at times. You become aware that what your parents or society has told you, or what school has taught you, is wrong and not always going to get you anywhere. You realize that having a significant other or material wealth doesn't mean you're happy. You realize that college or having a secure job doesn't guarantee success. You realize that most people are just trying to fake it until they make it, and that not all of the people in your life may be genuine. When you become aware at a young age, you realize how messed up and backwards this world is. The fact that people will judge you on the most basic things, like your looks, race, religion, sexual orientation, gender, etc. and not look any further is depressing. When you start to become aware of that superficiality, you wish that you could change it all, but you realize that you can't; and it's frustrating. It is easy to fall into a cycle of cynicism.

I will warn you, becoming aware may cost you your sanity. What I mean by that is that your ability to function in a "normal" society will be more difficult. You will realize that social hierarchies and social constructs are meaningless, and

CHAPTER TWELVE

you may choose to stop participating in and all out refuse them. You begin to realize that one of the functions of society itself is to exploit the use of authority and control or a lack thereof. Questioning authority figures should be a normal and safe part of living in a moral society, but when your questioning reveals that the authority figures are in fact not moral, you realize that they cannot hold any real power over you. In these conversations with my friends, I learned that we have so much power, and the way we think creates our perception of reality. Each day since, I have learned to be aware of what mindset I am in. I catch myself self-sabotaging or hyper-focusing on a topic of thought every now and then—it happens, and that is normal. People may say that this is crazy or a mentally unstable way of thinking, and that's fair but inaccurate. If those people would like to say that believing you are so much more powerful than you've been conditioned to believe is crazy, then baby, call me crazy.

Some things cannot be changed until people decide to change it within themselves. As individual human beings, we are each living in our individual realities. That is why I cannot say that I completely understand your perspective, and you cannot completely understand mine—you have never walked a mile in my shoes, and vice versa. Everything in this universe is made up of energy which cannot be created or destroyed, but simply changed or transferred. There is a phrase that goes something like, "If you want to see a change in the world, you first have to make that change within yourself." If you put the energy in to make a change within your surroundings, that change is ultimately going to cause an effect on the world at large, in some way. Similarly, the actions of others have consequences that eventually may have an effect on you. We are products of our circumstances, but sometimes, there are circumstances we cannot control. However, we can control how we respond to them and how we allow them to impact our perception.

We are all connected. We are one. Not only "we" as humans, but *we* as in all living things and things that exist, from animals to plants to anything that radiates or emits energy in this universe. I believe that we are all an expression of *life*, mosaics of the people who have crossed our paths and of those who laid the foundation for us to walk on before we were born.

Going back to this idea that we are all one, when I was growing up Catholic, I was taught that God is all around us, everywhere, and within us all the time. This was a concept that resonated with me then, and still resonates with me now. However, I believe that as we are all an expression of *life*, we are also an expression of God (or Allah, a Higher Power, the Universe, or whatever your name for it is; I believe we are all describing the same immortal power). When I look at my own life, the power that I have to curate my own reality, I am always in awe when I think to think about how the complexity I see within my own experience is there within the lives of every human that I meet. And with every human being I meet, I am witnessing and interacting with another manifestation of God. I personally use the term "the Universe" more so than "God," but in my belief, they are interchangeable. You are the Universe experiencing itself. You are so much greater than what you've been taught. The parts of you that some may call weird or different, are what make your expression of God unique, so embrace it; you're not crazy.

One thing my friends and I did on that walk in the forest, but also at other points throughout our weekend trip, was meditate. Breathwork and deep meditation, which I have found to be extremely beneficial, can often lead to spiritual transformation. Some people, including myself, would describe the transformation I had on that trip as a Spiritual Awakening. My eyes were opened to some of the most magical, complex aspects of life that are so subtle many people never see them. Taking a step back and looking at the big picture from an unfamiliar perspective allowed me to truly understand how we are all connected. Looking at my own life from a greater perspective also helped me come to new realizations about myself.

Some people use drugs, and especially psychedelics, to come to new realizations about their lives, and I can understand why. When you're in an altered state of consciousness, you have these epiphanies and great ideas, because breakthroughs happen in non-ordinary, non-conforming states of consciousness. When we're in our normal ordinary consciousness, we see things in the way we've always seen them, and it becomes a pattern in our awareness. But when we alter our consciousness, we alter our perspective in order to see it from a different angle. I do not condone reckless drug or psychedelic use. However, when treated with the utmost respect, transformation on the grandest scale can occur when used responsibly. I know there will be people who read this chapter and scoff at the idea of "drugs" being used for a "spiritual" purpose. I understand their perspective, because I too was raised and conditioned to believe that all drugs are bad; however, before you make any rash judgments, I ask you to open your mind and your heart.

It is important for me to state here that one does not need to use psychedelics to experience a non-ordinary state of consciousness or spiritual transformation, but it can be a catalyst. The way they manifest in each individual's perception of the world is different, and one must treat that with respect. It is absolutely possible, and quite easy, to have an awfully unpleasant experience if you are not careful. You need to be clear about what your intentions are for using them beforehand. The goal is not to "escape reality" or to say "fuck you" to the people who do not understand the spiritual and medicinal benefits; the goal is to see your reality from a unique perspective while understanding that that state of consciousness cannot be your reality all of the time.

In the end, I saw my life from a completely different perspective, and my eyes were opened to other ways of thinking. Because I was able to see myself in a new light, I was able to express compassion towards myself and the mistakes I had made in my past. I understood how I had done the best I could, with the circumstances I was given and the mindset I had been conditioned into. Ultimately, I learned that it takes one person to forgive and two to reconcile. But what about when the relationship that needs reconciling is the one with yourself?

Love is a powerful form of energy. Other people can show us love and teach us more about it, but until we understand what it means to love ourselves, we cannot truly understand its power. And that *power* is what turns a person's dreams into their reality, because until then, that's all that they are: a dream.

Questions to Contemplate:

1. **What season best describes the phase I'm in right**

now? Why?
2. **What do I believe in? Where do these beliefs come from? What does religion or spirituality mean to me?**
3. **How do I ground myself? What or who keeps me sane?**

IV

EMBRACING UNCERTAINTY

13

CHAPTER THIRTEEN

NOTE: This chapter discusses the topics of substance abuse and eating disorders.

After my relationship with Evan ended, I wasn't sure if we could ever be friends. We had several mutual friends at the time, so I figured at least being civil would be the best route to take. It was kind of awkward at first, but eventually it started to feel like we were actually building somewhat of a friendship. We never spent time together on our own because the thought of it made me feel uncomfortable, and I didn't want him to think that I still had feelings for him. *What were his thoughts about staying in touch or having so many mutual friends? Did this make him uncomfortable?* Sometimes it felt like the comments he would make and his actions, in true narcissistic fashion, manipulated how I viewed him as a person after that. They say actions speak louder than words, but at the time, I wasn't listening that closely.

In the spring of my junior year, most of my friends left to study abroad. When I think back to that semester, it brings back emotions and memories for me, both positive and negative. That was definitely a semester where I explored deeper into my identity, but in the process, I was also closing myself off to a lot of what I was experiencing to try and cope. Solitude and isolation can be dangerous spaces to be in when you are not in a stable place mentally. During that time, I would check in on Evan fairly frequently, because I knew he wasn't in a healthy headspace and most of his friends were gone as well. *Did he feel as alone as I did sometimes? How was he coping with his own struggles?* I didn't want him to feel like he was completely isolated or like that he didn't have anyone to go to.

With my closest friends being in different countries, I had the opportunity to branch out and strengthen many of the friendships I had with people that I was not always able to hang out with before. It was such a fun time building those newer friendships, and I am grateful to have had that time to establish connections with people outside of my typical friend group. The friends you make in college are truly some of the most fun friendships. While I knew at the time that many of them would not be lifelong friends, the fact that our paths crossed, even if only for a couple of years, was something that I am eternally grateful for. Those people are some of the coolest human beings I've met. But towards the end of that semester, my whole world was rocked, redefining the word "friendship" for me.

One day, Evan blocked me on Snapchat and refused to acknowledge me. *What prompted this? Why was this the course of action he decided to take?* Up until that point, we hadn't talked much, but any time I did send him a message, he usually didn't open it for days and said that there was something weird going

CHAPTER THIRTEEN

on with his account, where he didn't get messages right away. Red flag. I suppose I should've taken the hint then, but the thought of losing him as a "friend" hurt, so I continued to reach out.

This is where I want to address the idea of being "toxic." The odds are pretty high that you have encountered someone, at some point in your life, who exhibits toxic behaviors, whether it be a "friend," family member, co-worker, authority figure etc. It can be difficult to identify a person with toxic qualities at first, because it usually requires you to distinguish between feelings of love, respect, and friendship and feelings of guilt, manipulation, and shame. People who are good at manipulation are usually particularly good at using their words and actions to confuse, disarm, and manipulate you to feel a certain way about them or a situation.

So, how did I identify that he was a toxic person in my life? Well, it definitely wasn't easy, I can tell you that much. The first indication was the feeling I had after hanging out with him. As an introverted person, I get my energy from being alone; being around other people is usually exhausting to me. However, the exhaustion I felt after talking to or being around him was different. Not only did I feel mentally drained, but I also felt emotionally wiped out. I wasn't always able to pinpoint exactly why I felt this way more often after hanging out with him than with other people, but I felt in my gut that there was something off. Because he was struggling mentally, I often felt sorry for him and responsible for making sure he was okay—also a sign to me that this was not a person I should want to be around. Of course, denial and the lack of ability to apologize or take accountability for anything were also indicators.

In myself, I noticed subtle changes in my behavior that were also indications that I was being manipulated, whether it was conscious or unconscious manipulation. I would often make excuses for his behavior and believed him when he told me lies that didn't add up, such as the "error" with his Snapchat account. I often felt unheard or not valued as a friend, which made me question my own viewpoint and worth. I noticed that my thoughts would sometimes be consumed with his opinions or that I was walking on eggshells around what I perceived his opinion to be. Like many others, I didn't realize I was being manipulated until it was too late—the manipulation had pushed me to do things I wouldn't normally ever do.

After he blocked me, I found out from one of our mutuals that he had been manipulating me the whole semester, and he had roped some of his "friends" into it as well. *Why? What was he trying to accomplish? Why block me after all of that?* I remember sitting on my friend Leigh's couch crying, because I didn't understand how a person could treat another human being so horribly. In that moment, I knew that she was a ride-or-die, because she kept it real with me. At that point, I knew he was a toxic person for me to have in my life, but she also helped me realize that my own behavior in that "friendship" had also been toxic. It felt like my heart was breaking all over again.

Given the right circumstances, I think it is possible for any person to become "toxic" in a relationship, no matter the perceived depth or type of that relationship. Especially if you haven't done the work to shine a light on the shadows in your past and work through any unhealed trauma, you can be more susceptible to manipulation and attracting "toxic" people into your life. This is primarily because toxic people take advantage of weak or nonexistent boundaries. If you grew

CHAPTER THIRTEEN

up in a comparable situation like I did, where "boundaries" were not something you were taught or encouraged to have, it can be difficult to unlearn codependent behaviors and learn how to set healthy boundaries. When I went on a healing, self-love journey that summer after, I truly learned what this all meant, but I'll describe that in Chapter 14.

***

If I am going to be honest and vulnerable in sharing my story, it is important for me to open a conversation about drug and alcohol abuse in college age people and how it is so normalized in our society. During my time in college, I can recount occasions where I genuinely had to question if someone I knew was struggling with an addiction or had a problem of overconsumption and if I needed to intervene and get help.

Going to college in the United States is an interesting experience. There is almost this fantasy that people have about what the college experience is or should be. Don't get me wrong, I had a lot of fun in college, but the "college experience" is overhyped in my opinion, and dangerously so.

At that age, you are learning how to take care of yourself in the most basic ways, such as cooking yourself meals, doing your own laundry, managing your finances, processing your emotions in a healthy way, etc. If you grew up in a household where you didn't have healthy examples of this, then wow, are those first few years of adulthood difficult. Even when it comes to time management for completing homework, working a job, taking care of your mental health, etc., when you've got a lot on your plate. It's easy to feel the stress and pressure to have it all figured out. Now I didn't have the same experiences as you, and vice versa, so there may be things that came easier to me than for you, and I can't speak for all young adults. But what I can say is that regardless of the examples you had growing up of "how to be an adult," when it's finally your turn, it's not easy. The most important thing I had to learn was the importance of structure and routine, simply for maintaining my sanity.

At first, this took the form of creating a consistent workout routine and eating healthier, unprocessed foods. While my intentions were good with paying more attention to my lifestyle choices, it slowly turned into something that was very unhealthy. My mindset with working out was that if my mind and my heart were going to be metaphorically sore, the rest of my body would be physically. I was pushing my body to learn how to fall and get back up again, in hopes that my mind and heart would do the same. My goal was never to lose weight; I wanted to build muscle, but my eating habits did not reflect that. When I was under pressure, sometimes my appetite would completely disappear. Many of my closest friends were not in the country, and the schedules of my friends who were still on campus didn't always line up with mine. This made it difficult for me to actually go to the dining halls to eat a meal. When I became aware of these patterns starting to form, I was genuinely afraid that I had developed an eating disorder. I never wanted to hurt myself, and I knew that I had to eat something to give my body fuel. There were times when my dinner would consist of a small plate place of only a couple carrots and cucumbers plus a tiny pile of lettuce, a bowl of sugary cereal, and maybe half of a banana. I realized that working out and burning way more calories than I was eating had become unhealthy coping mechanisms for me that closed my eyes to what the real issues were that I was going through.

Especially given the circumstance of dealing with a toxic

friendship s that semester, dealing with a toxic friendship, I was trying to cope with, and, honestly, numb the stressful emotions that I was experiencing. One of my close friends at the time was also going through some mental and emotional hardship that led him to turn to alcohol as an escape, and he is not alone in this. Many college kids turn to alcohol as a coping mechanism, while other people I knew turned to drugs to numb the internal turmoil they were experiencing. We could use the excuse that it was all for fun in the moment, and honestly, it was; but in truth, we were all just trying our best to get by, live another day. I do not regret any of those moments or the memories made, because even though most of us were coping with *something*, we were coping *together*. I knew that some of the decisions I or my friends were making were not exactly healthy, but when you feel like there is so much that is out of your control, you try to find that feeling of control somewhere else. During those few months of my junior year, I saw sides of myself and of my friends that I don't think any of us knew existed. Versions of ourselves that we had tried so hard to keep pushed down, but inevitably came out the more we tried to push.

Despite our unhealthy habits, these people felt more like a family to me than my own blood, because we were able to have some of the most raw, honest, deep conversations about our own demons. There was a phrase that we often used, "Everyone eats in this family." This phrase didn't just apply to literal food either. We had each other's backs and did our best to take care of everyone physically, emotionally, mentally, etc. because we were all going through some challenging times.

I definitely thought that it would be easier to blame a substance or another person, but blame does not change how you feel or what happened. I cannot blame myself for how I felt or the way I acted. Playing the blame game helps no one. I learned that I cannot blame another person for awakening a version of myself that has always been there; I realized that she needed to heal in more ways than one, and that she needed to be loved.

Addiction is a scary thing to experience and to witness your friends and family struggling with. I honestly believe that at the core of every addiction is a wounded child, a child who is in a constant state of craving. When we are children, we seek approval from our parents, because they are the ones responsible for providing for our basic needs, both physically and emotionally. As we grow older, if those needs are not met, we seek out approval elsewhere, such as from our peers or romantic partners. Now that social media is such a prevalent part of our society, people also seek out that approval online. Addiction does not just take the form of alcohol or drugs; it can also take the form of a dopamine addiction that comes from instant gratification and online validation.

When we seek out approval, we are communicating multiple things. One being that our relationship with ourselves is not stable, and another being that our basic need for human connection is not being met. Parasocial interactions and connections with people online can lead to superficial beliefs of friendships or relationships. When this translates into the physical world, this can look like people having fun with their friends, but not genuinely enjoying the company of them. It can also look like talking about things that are important to you with your partner, but not fully feeling heard or like you can trust that person's response. This desire for approval and the stress that comes with not having our basic need for human connection met can lead to a person to turn turning toward a temporary form of relief. And this desire, craving, yearning, or whatever you want to call it, can be traced back to how we felt as a child.

I do not believe that cannabis is a gateway drug, or that alcohol, nicotine, caffeine or even dopamine are a gateway to addiction. Trauma is the gateway. It can take the form of neglect or absent parents, physical or emotional abuse in one's childhood, sexual assault, witnessing violence, etc. Addiction does not simply cause violent behavior, drug or substance abuse, self-harm, or even hypersexuality. In my experience, these are often the symptoms of much bigger issues that cause a person to turn towards and attach onto some form of relief. And it almost always stems from a wounded child with a past involving some form of trauma. Most people do not take the time to consider this, especially when it comes to alcoholism and drug addiction among college-age people, because it is deemed a "normal" part of the college experience. What many people fail to communicate is empathy. They say that everything is good in moderation, but it is easier than you may realize for that seemingly harmless habit to turn into a dangerous addiction. I have heard horrible things said about people who are alcoholics or drug addicts without them realizing that their own friends or children could one day be in an addict's shoes.

If I've learned anything from those experiences with toxic relationships and using drugs or alcohol to cope, it's that the people around you are always going through their own struggles, and they may not have your best interest in mind. I have a lot of love for the people who were truly my friends during that time, but I also had to reconsider the way that I defined and perceived forgiveness—forgiving others, but most importantly, forgiving myself.

If there's anything you take away from this chapter, let it be this: there are going to be times where life is really fucking hard, and you won't understand why you're being put through it. You may not recognize yourself or the people around you, and those moments are difficult, because it makes you question everything you've known, everything you thought was safe and secure. But in those moments when you are seeing those darker sides of yourself, where you are feeling those scarier emotions, in my experience, it really helped me to cling on to the idea that this is all temporary, that the present moment is never permanent. When I've been in a darker place, Jade has always reminded me, "The only thing that never changes is that everything always changes."

Questions to Contemplate:

1. **What is the first thing I turn to when I am struggling? Is it truly helpful?**
2. **What is a memory I wish to forget but can't?**
3. **What is a lie I continue to tell myself? Why is it difficult for me to be honest with myself?**

14

CHAPTER FOURTEEN

After the rough semester to close out my junior year, I was in an interesting emotional state. I was feeling very snubbed, forgotten, pushed away, and overall, treated like garbage. That summer, I decided to focus not only on healing from that situation, but also learning how to forgive. I first had to forgive myself for how I handled and coped with the situation, as well as for allowing him to manipulate me the way he did.

Honestly, I remember going into the summer of 2019 not really knowing what to expect. I had made a lot of big plans for that summer that included traveling to Leipzig, Germany, for a three-week education seminar. The program was part of a research grant which helped to inform a research project that I completed the next year. The time that I spent in Germany was such a great period of personal growth for myself and my language skills.

Before the program started, I experienced one of the biggest anxiety attacks of my life. I remember sitting in the room that I was staying in, trembling in fear. This is what I mean when

I say that my eye disorder can cause me anxiety. Traveling to unfamiliar places and having to rely on the vision and knowledge that I have can be incredibly stressful, and at times, it has made traveling very difficult. At that moment, I was worried that I would not be able to find where I was supposed to meet everyone else the next day to begin our program. There were 20+ people from around the United States who would be attending this seminar, and I did not know any of them beforehand. I was worried and insecure about finding the meeting location and that I would make a bad first impression if I arrived late because of it. Eventually, I was able to regain control of my thoughts and calm myself down, but throughout those three weeks, my mental strength was definitely tested.

Being in Germany also gave me the literal space I needed to come to terms with many of my insecurities. I had traveled across an ocean entirely on my own, to a country that spoke a language that I was not completely fluent in. I was not a stranger to doing things that pushed me out of my comfort zone. After having that anxiety attack and seeing how much I had transformed internally after this trip, I made the commitment to myself to continue doing things that scared me, because I realized that there would always be a stronger version of myself on the other side.

What I love about traveling is experiencing a way of life that is different from your own. Even in cultures that are familiar or similar to the ones you are used to, there is always something new to be learned and a new perspective to be seen. During those three weeks, I was able to travel to a few different cities throughout Germany with the program and meet unique people along the way.

CHAPTER FOURTEEN

I also had the opportunity to squeeze in a visit to two of my friends who were completing internships in Augsburg, Germany; one of those friends was Eleanor. I had only one day throughout my time in Germany where I was not doing anything for my seminar, and I knew I wanted to visit them because why the hell not? If the only thing separating us is distance, I will travel to see my friends. I was there for less than 24 hours, but it was 100% worth it, and I am so glad that I was able to spend the day with them.

That day trip was a key part of my healing process. I had not seen Eleanor in over five months, because she went straight from studying in South Africa to her internship in Germany. I had not had the opportunity to properly fill her in on what had happened while she was gone. While we were waiting for our other friend to wake up, she and I got breakfast, sat in the city center, and then went to a park to catch up. I explained to her what had happened from my perspective and, but acknowledged that his was probably quite different, but still valid. She gave me some insightful advice and held space for me to vocally process everything. It was still going to be some time before I was able to emotionally and mentally process it all, but that day was the first step in allowing myself to get everything out of my system without feeling judged.

**

When I returned home from that trip, I immediately went to work at a summer camp in the middle of the woods in northern Minnesota. This whole summer was a period of complete sobriety for me, from alcohol, drugs, nicotine, everything. It was a time for me to really clear my head and clear my heart. I needed that time in that space to take a break. I made a lot of really special connections throughout that time that I hope to have in my life for a while. It was a fresh start, and I needed to be on my own away from anyone who already had preconceived ideas about me.

My time spent there was so therapeutic, and the people who came into my life then, came at exactly the right time. They unconsciously helped me along the way during my journey of healing and taught me a whole new perspective on what love is and looks like, as well as what it means to set boundaries for your own mental health and prosperity. The most important lesson I learned that summer was what it feels like to genuinely love the life you are living, as well as the personal power that comes with forgiving yourself and others.

I had made mistakes that I wasn't even conscious of during my junior year, but when I realized what I had done to contribute to the situation, it was hard not to judge myself for making those mistakes. I think that the type of mental manipulation I experienced really does something to a person and how they communicate, interact, and form relationships with other people and themselves.

When I first arrived at camp and started bonding with the people there, I remember feeling hesitant to share myself with them fully. We were connecting on a deep level, which is kind of inevitable when you spend 24/7 with people in the middle of the forest, but I noticed myself pushing back. I was afraid that if I let too many people in too quickly that it would be hard for me to give myself the space I needed to heal. But I realized that sometimes, you have to lean into that fear and trust the process. That fear was there for a reason; and those people were there to challenge me to overcome my hesitations about connecting with others, despite negative experiences with another person.

CHAPTER FOURTEEN

As soon as I let go of control and released my fear of connecting deeply with other human beings, I realized how powerful genuine human connection is, no matter how long or short your time with them is. During my seven weeks of working at that camp, I made so many amazing memories and friendships that I will cherish for the rest of my life. But most importantly, I overcame my fear of connection, learned how to set boundaries, and I forgave myself.

When you have your heart broken, you realize that you're not actually broken; you've just had some really soul crushing things happen to you. You've experienced heavy emotions and seen some of the darkest parts of yourself. But at the end of the day, I had to look myself in the mirror and come to terms with the fact that the person I was before is not the person who I am or who I am going to be. She is a part of me for sure, but each day is an opportunity to grow and become the person I want to be, despite the opinions and actions of another person. My previous choices and decisions on other days do not have to dictate my actions today. Just because there have been times in my life where I have been insecure, or where I have been judgmental of myself, or where I have fallen into self-destructive tendencies, that doesn't mean I have to choose those behaviors every single day, which is part of learning to love yourself and every version of you that has existed.

Healing is not a linear process. There were times when I felt like I had regressed back to old habits, but every time I tried to get back on my path towards healing, I realized that "healing" is not something to search for. It lives within the fabric of humanity, in the moments we decide to try again another day, despite relapsing the day before. It is in the moments when we become aware of things we previously didn't even notice. It is in the moments when we decide to repair after we've been hurt, or we've hurt someone else. It is in the moments we choose not to break the promises to ourselves or give up when something is hard. It is in the moments when we decide to try, even when the uncertainty of failure is daunting. It is in the moments when we realize that everything we have gone through until this point has gotten us to this moment. It is in the moments when we choose our happiness above our suffering—whatever that means to you.

There were times when I tried running away from my feelings when they came up, but what I learned is that no matter how fast or how far I run, those feelings will always stay buried if I don't uncover them. That summer, I was in a safe place where I could let those feelings rise to the surface. I was hurt and disappointed in the way Evan treated me and the way I handled that pain. Learning how to let go of the blame I had for myself allowed me to see that that the pain he caused me was a result of the pain he was feeling within himself. It never mattered how much I or anyone else cared for him, because he did not care for himself.

Forgiveness is a lot more complicated than simply apologizing. And I knew that I wouldn't be getting one of those any time soon; so eventually, I forgave him for how he treated me; but most importantly, I forgave myself. I had found peace in the idea that he would no longer be a part of my life.

***

When I came back to begin my senior year, all of my closest friends knew what he had done and how he treated me. I didn't have to avoid him, life naturally took care of that; however, there were a couple times when my friends would tell me about

CHAPTER FOURTEEN

how he was doing or what he was up to. They had also told me that he had said he felt horrible for how things happened last year, but he didn't make any attempt to let me know that until later in the semester.

One night, I was going out to the bars with my friends. We walked in, and we were putting our coats away. My friend Leigh came up behind me and whispered in my ear, "Amanda, Evan wants to talk to you. He's coming up now." I didn't know what to do; I was honestly paralyzed by the fact that he wanted to talk to me at all. I turned around, and there he was. He began by saying that he was so terribly sorry for how he treated me, and he wanted us to be able to move past this. He felt bad for what he did and that I didn't deserve to be treated that way.

In that moment, while he was talking, I was flabbergasted that I was hearing what I was from him. He is not the type of person to apologize for anything. ANYTHING. So, to hear those words coming out of his mouth did not feel real. When he finished talking, I told him that I appreciated his apology and that I had forgiven him a while ago. He asked if he could hug me, and we did. I will never forget how I felt in that moment while we were hugging. There were so many emotions going through me at that time. I was happy that I finally had the closure and peace I had been hoping for. I was also a little proud of him because I knew how hard it must've been to swallow his pride.

The rest of the night, my friend group hung out again like old times. We were back on our bullshit, to say the least. We walked to Kwik Trip to get some munchies, stole a sidewalk blocker (which we eventually put back at the end of the semester), and laughed the night away in our apartment to close out the night. It was nice to know that we had both made our peace and could move through our individual healing. I hope that one day, he is able to look himself in the mirror and be happy with who he sees, because he is the reason that I believe that people can change.

***

Living with trauma is hard, but it is even harder when it pops back up later and you're trying to come to terms with it. Sometimes you can do everything right and try to set yourself up to have a good day, and then you face something that you haven't faced in a long time. It brings up all of those emotions again. When your body has these emotional responses, it is important to release it so it isn't bottled up or suppressed within your nervous system, but that can sometimes throw your entire day off. And for anyone who goes through this, it's important to be proud of yourself for having the courage to face things that are really hard. Do not feel guilty if you need to reward yourself with a nap or maybe not working for too long that day, or even just lying in your bed and crying it out—crying is the body's expression of healing. It's not easy, and you're not alone.

I love seeing people talk about spreading positivity and being a light in this world; we need more of it. However, it's also important to remember that the human experience is so much more complex. As we ascend and become increasingly more aware of this, I believe that we also need people and minds that are capable and equipped to sit and be in that complexity. We need minds that can be centered and open to the full range of what humans have the ability to experience. We need minds that can appreciate the range of nuance that comes with human life, while also experiencing the great polarity that comes with it. These minds are not only capable of spreading positivity, but also capable of empowering it within others.

I would like to conclude this chapter with a sentiment to how freeing it is to forgive yourself and others. Forgiveness is a beautiful thing, and I sometimes feel that people misinterpret its significance. It's not something that you do for others; it's something you do for yourself. It is a sense of acknowledging the pain and suffering that someone has caused you, while also understanding that they are human. We all make mistakes; and forgiving someone is a reminder to yourself that you too are human. Forgiving someone is not about opening the door for them to mistreat you again; it is closing that door within yourself to never *allow* it again.

I have so much peace, love, and joy for this time period in my life, because it is when I first fell in love with myself—I will never take that for granted. I know that for so many people, learning to love yourself is one of the hardest things to do. At the time this was all occurring, I felt vastly different than I do now. Overcoming insecurities and emotional wounds is difficult to do on your own, because the mind is a powerful place; and it requires even more power to change its thought patterns. While I began to understand what it meant to love myself during this time, I was also forced to face some of my deepest fears and insecurities.

Questions to Contemplate:

1. **What does forgiveness mean to me?**
2. **What do I need to forgive myself for? What do I need to forgive others for?**
3. **Think of a situation or person that was difficult for**

me to move on from. Why was it difficult to move on? What fears or emotions came up when trying to let go?

CHAPTER FIFTEEN

My biggest fear at the moment is to be mute
Trapped inside my own head
With no way of getting my thoughts out
No way of feeling grounded
No way of feeling connected
No way of feeling safe
I feel like I have been muted by my own mind
Like my thoughts are not meant to be heard
Like the actions I contribute are not seen or felt
Like the people around me are not real
I feel scared
I'm scared of feeling trapped
I'm scared to grow up
I'm scared to wake up in a life that wasn't created by me
-a stream of consciousness

At the beginning of my senior year, my friends and I decided to go on another weekend trip. On this trip, I experienced a lot of anxiety, and at times, it felt like I was literally trapped inside my own head. I felt like I could not communicate what I was thinking or how I was feeling into words. I would say something to my friends, but it didn't match what I felt or thought. We went into town that night, and I felt trapped and unsafe. I separated myself from our group and went to sit by myself to try and come down from the anxiety. I sat on a bench underneath the light of a lamp post in a nearby park, breathing in and out, reminding myself that this was all temporary—the anxiety would soon pass.

I began thinking about all I hoped to accomplish one day and the dreams I wanted to make a reality. It scared me. Not the thought of me *not* achieving those things, but the thought of me actually doing all that scared me. Honestly, it scares me still today. It is the main reason why writing this book was challenging. I think, subconsciously, on that trip, I knew I would one day write a book. I want to say the right words, convey the right messages, and when I say "right," I mean "right" for me, as in speaking my truth. I know that to some, my message may not resonate, and that's okay. One day, my words or actions may become problematic in the eyes of society; and I am okay with that because in this moment, I am genuinely expressing myself. As I continue to learn and grow as a person, my *truth* or perspective will also evolve.

I learned on that trip that one of my biggest fears is to be mute or feel like I cannot speak. While I hesitate to use my voice, something I learned as a child, I do this because I know it's one of my strengths. I know the power I have in my voice and how I articulate my words. That is part of my fear. I have been scared, at times, to use my voice, but I don't want to lose or silence it anymore. When Mr. J. said to not be a sponge, I took that to mean that I can't keep everything to myself if

CHAPTER FIFTEEN

it can help others. These next few stories that I share were the manifestation of my biggest fear coming to life. They are some of the most valuable lessons that I've learned.

During this time of my life, I was going through a lot of change and transformation. I feel like not a lot of people ever talk about this part: where you're no longer a caterpillar and not quite yet a butterfly. You don't know who you are, or where you're going, or what you want to do with your life. All you know is that every fiber in your being is calling for transformation, for disruption, for a revolution of the ego. On that trip, it felt like a part of my ego died. But this was not the death of *me*; this was the death of who I once was. All I had to do was surrender to the growing pains, because the transition from a caterpillar to a butterfly is more painful than it is beautiful.

***

Throughout my education program in college, I was required to complete a certain number of hours volunteering in classrooms. My senior year, I took a class that focused specifically on the pedagogy of teaching a world language. For this class, I had to complete a practicum in a German class at a local high school. This high school was in a rural town outside of the main city, and the demographic of the area reflected that. I was familiar with this demographic, because it was remarkably similar, both in terms of socioeconomic background and size, to the area I grew up in.

While volunteering at this school, I worked with a teacher who, in many ways, reminded me of a version of myself or a version of myself that I could potentially grow into if I wasn't careful. She was introspective and introverted, but also cynically opinionated and judgmental. She had been teaching at that school for over a decade, so she was very comfortable in her classroom. Her students on the other hand, I could not say the same.

It wasn't that they were uncomfortable with her, but they expressed to me many times that she did not always respond well to their questions when they asked for help. There was never really a genuine moment for me to connect with the kids, except for when I taught a lesson on my own for my professor to come and observe. During class, I did my best to explain concepts of the German language, and I even taught them tricks to remember things like conjugation and cases. When they used these methods in class, I could sense that their teacher was a little frustrated that they were not using *her* method as often. *How did she feel in those moments? What was she observing? Could I have asked her for more feedback? Was I wrong to encourage students to use my method if it helped them more?* She never expressed any discontent with me about this, but I could feel that I was possibly overstepping.

For a couple years in college, I was a teaching assistant for a professor in the German Department at my university. She was an old-fashioned, respected professor, but in my opinion, she was very stuck in her way of teaching. Most of the work I did for her was organizational and completed outside of class time. I had a busy schedule but was willing to be available to attend as many of her classes as she would allow. One day in particular, I remember she was teaching her class about the difference between the prepositions *nach* and *zu* when describing going "to" somewhere. As the students were working on an assignment, I was talking with a small group of them who were struggling to remember the difference between the two. I taught them a way to think about and visually conceptualize the difference. When the professor I was assisting overheard this, rather than pulling me aside or speaking with me after class, she announced to the whole class, "Amanda, you are not the teacher in this room, you are the assistant." *What prompted her to do this? How was she thinking/feeling in that moment? Why did she think this was the way to communicate this?* This is a memory that stuck with me long after that class was over. I am sure that this professor did not think anything of it, but it greatly impacted the way I perceived her from that moment on.

So, when I was in this classroom volunteering with a teacher for my practicum, I was very hesitant to overstep her boundary as the teacher in the room. I told her that because of this previous experience, I was hesitant about overstepping with her, but I do not think she understood how much of an impact it actually had on me. I felt that she had not clearly communicated her expectations of me until we debriefed afterwards.

During one of her classes, she was asking her students what plans they had for the weekend, and one student mentioned going to a local grocery store on the other side of town. This teacher responded with, "Oh, you mean the *ghetto* one?" *What did she just say? Did I hear that right? Why did she choose to use that word?*

Being an advocate for my students is something that I am continuously working on, which requires continuing to learn about them as individuals and about the backgrounds that they come from. Many of the students in this class laughed when she said that and confirmed that they knew exactly which store she was talking about by describing some of the people who typically shop there. Immediately, I felt my face getting warm and my ears started ringing. I knew I had to say something, but I did not know what to say or how to say it, so I did not say anything during class.

However, I knew in my soul that I could not walk out of that room without talking to this teacher about why that word probably should not have been used to describe that store in her classroom. Many people in the United States use the term "ghetto" to refer to more impoverished, lower income areas, which is also usually a way for them to refer to communities of people who have been historically excluded and marginalized, such as communities of members in a minority group. In this specific situation, I knew that was what they were referring to because of the descriptions the students used. This is a word in which the definition and use has been reclaimed and changed over the years, especially during the time of American segregation and after.

However, in a classroom where students are learning about the German language, history, and culture, I believe it is also important for them to understand how this word was used in Germany during the Holocaust and in other regions of the world, like Italy, to describe parts of the city where Jewish people lived. During the Holocaust, the Nazis established *ghettos* to hold populations of Jewish people to separate, exploit, and eventually kill them ("Ghettos"). Knowing this history, I felt that it was insensitive and inappropriate to casually throw that word around without providing the context of how the word has been used against people within minority groups.

Afterwards, I approached the teacher, and I asked her why she chose to use that word to describe the store the student had mentioned. She said that it was a term they had used in the past, and so she was trying to relate to them. *Okay, but why* that *word specifically? Are there better ways to relate to them?* When I mentioned how this could be potentially harmful to other students in the school or the local communities as well as insensitive to the history in a German context, she disagreed and said that I did not understand the demographic of the area where I was; but I did, and that was the problem.

Over 97% of the students in that classroom were White. I expressed to her that I felt it was wrong to perpetuate this idea in her classroom, and this is where I definitely overstepped her boundaries, because the way I approached this conversation was not in the most respectful manner. *How did that make her feel? Could I have handled it differently or given her the benefit of the doubt?* I mentioned my point of how I felt that in a German classroom, it was especially inappropriate to casually use this word and perpetuate the negative connotations to her students, when there could have been an opportunity for learning there.

After expressing these points, the teacher didn't say much more than, "Okay." *What was she really thinking? Was I offensive in how I addressed my concerns? How did I make her feel?* I left the classroom, and that was the last time I was there. Immediately, I emailed my professor, and I explained what had happened. She responded, asking if I would like to video call to debrief and talk about the situation when I returned back to my apartment on campus.

When we did a video call, she told me that this teacher had also emailed her about what had happened, and she offered me some perspective from that teacher. The teacher said she felt that I was very disrespectful and rude. My professor reassured me that she would always be on my side in any situation, but especially in a situation involving racism, because it is not often that someone is confronted on their racism, and they don't walk away feeling a little attacked in the situation. When I look back on this, I completely agree with this teacher that I could have handled the situation so much better than I did, but I did not know how to handle it any better at the time; and honestly, I do not regret what I said.

My professor suggested that I send her an email to apologize for how I acted, if I felt that I was in the wrong. However, she also encouraged me to stand behind my beliefs, but to do so in a respectful manner if a situation like this ever occurred in her classroom again. She said that I had the option to terminate my practicum at this school early, if I felt that it was not a productive place for me to be. I said that I would be willing to return to the classroom, because I did not want this to impact my own education. *What could I still learn from this experience?* The next morning, I received an email from the teacher I was volunteering with that said I was no longer welcome in her classroom or at the school. She also said that I should possibly reconsider a career in education. *Was this just because of our last encounter or was there something else that made her think this?* This was reflected in how she rated my overall performance in her classroom; like I said, she did not have a good perception of me after that last meeting, so I had an idea of what was coming when she submitted my evaluation to my professor.

To this day, I am so grateful for the support of my professor and the Education Department during this time. Throughout this semester, I had been handling a lot of stressful circumstances, which I will describe a little bit later, and this professor was truly always in my corner. I'd also like to add that while this was all going on, my professor was on her way to a conference in a different state, and she took time out of her schedule to make sure that I was doing okay mentally. When I received my

CHAPTER FIFTEEN

evaluation and comments, my professor told me to take them all with a grain of salt, because she had seen me working in the classroom with students before and did not agree with many of the teacher's comments or ratings. However, my professor encouraged me to use this as a learning opportunity and to at least thank the teacher for the time I was able to spend in her classroom.

It is quite ironic actually, because on the first day in this teacher's classroom, she had talked to me about how she wanted to retire in a couple years and that I should apply to work at that school when she did—it is hard to find teachers for German programs in the United States, so she was worried the program would end when she retired. Well, I think it is safe to say that I probably don't have a good chance of getting that job now, even if I did want to work at that school.

Overall, I felt insignificant, incapable, inadequate, invisible, and underestimated after working with her. *Was this a projection of how this teacher felt her students viewed her?* Regardless, this was definitely a curve ball that knocked my confidence in myself and my capability down quite a bit.

***

I do not believe one can teach a lesson that they themselves have not learned. How to address instances of racism was a lesson that came back around for me during my first year of teaching. In one of the 8th grade classes, I taught with another teacher who was working from home, due to health concerns about returning to teach in person during a pandemic. During a couple of the classes, I noticed that she used the phrase, "any ole cotton-picking day." Again, the vast majority of the students in this classroom were White, and this is a phrase that doesn't have a place in a classroom, due to its reference to slavery in American history.

I knew that I needed to be more aware of how I was going to handle this situation when I addressed it with this teacher, especially because I respected her as a person and felt that she said it out of habit, not knowing how it could be perceived by her students. I wanted to talk with another teacher that I trusted about how to go about starting this conversation. I informed her of my previous experience at that school during my practicum in college, and she was shocked by how the other teacher reacted. She also reassured me that the person I was co-teaching with now would absolutely be more receptive to my feedback.

I waited until the next day to bring this up with my co-teacher, because I wanted to make sure I had a clear head and the right words to convey what I wanted to express to her. After we finished planning our lesson for the next day, I gently mentioned what she had said the day before and in other classes. I mentioned that especially given the current political and social climate of the United States at the time, what she said could be interpreted very negatively by students, parents, and others in the community. She confessed that she did not even remember using the phrase and said that it was something she had always heard her mother say, but in no way excused her behavior.

We had a very productive conversation and afterwards, she thanked me for bringing it to her attention and asked that I call her out on it in the future if I heard her use it again. In fact, she did use it again in another class, but immediately after saying it, she stopped herself, and said, "I don't know why I said that; that it is not an okay phrase for me to use to describe what I mean." She rephrased her sentence and continued with the class. After the students left the room, she was still on the video call. She said that she is now becoming more aware of how often she unconsciously uses that phrase.

That is the most important thing I want you to take away from this story. When confronted by someone about racism, it is not necessarily an attack on the *person* being racist, but an attack on the *racism* itself. I myself am unlearning many of the racist behaviors and thought patterns that I learned from growing up in this society but more specifically a rural Midwest town, because racism is systematic. It is something that we learn through how we operate in different systems in our society, whether that be in a system of education, justice, economics, etc.

The greatest lesson that I learned from this is that handling racism, especially in an educational setting, must always be done with have compassion and learning at the forefront. One cannot learn if they feel attacked. The difference between the two situations is that I did not have compassion for the teacher during my practicum. I did not give her the benefit of the doubt. By not having learning or compassion at the forefront, I completely closed off the possibility of a productive conversation. I learned that you could disagree with someone and have different opinions, but that doesn't change the other person's mind.

Life has an interesting way of teaching us lessons. You see, I believe that the Universe will keep putting you in situations to learn a lesson until you finally learn it. Thanks to my co-teacher at the time, and the teacher I spoke with prior, I have learned how to handle similar situations, whether it involves confronting racism, sexism, homophobia, ableism, classism, etc. Some may criticize the way I handled both of these situations, but I am still learning and far from perfect. I'm also always open to constructive criticism when I make a mistake. The important thing is, in the future, I now have a frame of reference to go back to as an example for how to bring up and have conversations about uncomfortable circumstances.

***

The fall semester of my senior year in college was a difficult one for me mentally. I had a lot on my plate that semester as I was finishing up my degree requirements for graduation prior to student-teaching in the next semester. On top of that, I was writing my senior thesis for my German degree, as well as conducting a research study within the German Department about how languages are taught and learned at the university level in the United States compared to in Germany. That being said, there was another experience I had this semester that rocked me to my core.

Financial insecurity is a real thing that many people face, especially young adults and college students. College in the United States is extremely and unnecessarily expensive, especially at private institutions like the one that I attended. If you are a first-generation student or someone who comes from a background that has not always been financially stable, there is a certain amount of stress that is always on your shoulders that your peers who grew up around people who pursued higher education or in financially secure situations cannot always understand.

One day, after volunteering in the classroom I mentioned at the beginning of this chapter, I noticed that I had a couple missed calls and a voicemail. When I got into my car, I listened to this voicemail in which someone told me that my identity and social security number had been compromised and I needed to contact the federal agency immediately. I wish I could say that I do not remember all the details of what happened next, but unfortunately, I remember it crystal clear as if it happened yesterday. And I can guess what you are thinking based on the minimal details I've given, "Amanda, why would you believe that a federal agency would have you contact them only over the phone about the situation?" I know, I know, I know. Trust me, hindsight is 20/20.

Basically, what happened next is I drove around to different gas stations, transferring my money onto gift cards, and giving the information to the "federal agency" that I was on the phone with, and they were able to take that money before I could realize what I was doing.

When I returned to my apartment and talked with my friends, they consoled me about the situation, but at the time, they also did not realize what was happening. At that point, I had not realized. It wasn't until after sitting in my room crying and thinking about the situation that I realized I had been scammed. I immediately called my parents and confessed that I fucked up BIG TIME! My mom started crying on the phone saying, "Oh, Amanda, how did you not realize what was going on?" But ultimately, and I expressed this to her as well, that I knew I fucked up, I knew it was stupid. She understood that fear has a powerful effect on people. I was frustrated after working in an environment where I wasn't valued, and this made it easier to control my emotions. I definitely wasn't in a clear headspace throughout the entire process of driving around transferring my money. She suggested that I go back to the gas stations where I had made these purchases and ask if it was too late to cancel them; and unfortunately, it was.

I'd like to give a shoutout to Leigh, again, truly a ride-or-die friend. She drove me around to these gas stations as I accepted the stupidity of my mistake and swallowed my pride to ask these people with humility and grace to help me in any way that they could (and they truly did try to help me). But despite my efforts, the money was gone.

Poof! Just like that, I had lost $1,200 of my hard-earned money. To some, that is not a lot, but that was ¾ of my savings, and I still had to pay for my licensure exams and language evaluations in order to apply for my teaching licenses the next semester, which cost me well over $400. So, add that on top of the financial insecurity I was already feeling at the time.

I learned many lessons from this experience. The first being that you should never trust someone claiming to be from a "federal agency" who is saying that your social security number and identity have been compromised. Which, duh, don't do that. Now I know and will never, ever make that mistake again. The second being that fear is, in my opinion, the most powerful emotion that can control a human being. If you are operating from a fear mindset, you cannot think clearly, and people with bad intentions will absolutely take advantage of that.

While talking on the phone with my dad the day after this all happened, he said that he had been in a similar situation when he was younger, and the same thing happened to him. I had also called the police the same night everything was going down, and they told me this happens to a lot of people, more than you'd probably think. Even though it was probably the most embarrassed that I've ever felt in my life, that is why I feel comfortable sharing this story with you. I know it was a mistake; and even in the thick of it all, I kept reminding myself that making mistakes doesn't have to be a bad thing, unless you learn nothing from them.

CHAPTER FIFTEEN

I think back to that day and count the infinite number of red flags about the situation, and I shake my head. I cannot change the decisions I made, but I am choosing to learn from the consequences. We all do stupid things. I guess if I want to preach about how you should make as many "mistakes" as you can in your twenties, I've gotta make a few myself too. Even if I were a dumbass in the moment, I could not continue to beat myself up over the situation. Money is a material thing that comes and goes, like energy in a tangible form. It has as much power as you give it.

Questions to Contemplate:

1. **When have I stood up for something I believe in? What was the outcome?**
2. **When have I kept quiet about something I disagreed with? Do I regret not speaking up?**
3. **What does vulnerability mean to me? What does it look or feel like? Who do I feel I can be vulnerable around? Why?**

16

CHAPTER SIXTEEN

I felt that in the previous semester, I had allowed my voice to be silenced. When I began my student teaching experience the following semester, I truly saw my potential as an educator. I completed my student teaching in a rural, small town school near my college, and it reminded me of the community that I grew up in. This community made me appreciate working in a small school, because it truly felt like a community.

Before I began my student teaching, I was very anxious about how I would do because of what had happened the previous semester and the comments that teacher had made about my ability to connect with students. But my mentor teacher for those few months of student teaching was an amazing example to me, and she reminded me of my high school German teacher. She taught me so much, and I am forever grateful to have had her as a support system and role model during that time.

My university supervisor, who was a former teacher at that school, was also such a positive support for me and provided me with valuable, constructive criticism. She used to be one of

CHAPTER SIXTEEN

the Speech coaches at the school as well, and she introduced me to one of the teachers there who was currently running the Speech team. We connected immediately, and she let me help coach some of the students. I was also able to judge one of the Speech meets. It felt like a full-circle moment for me, because being on the Speech team in middle school and high school was such an integral and transformative time in my life. Teaching at that school empowered me and made me feel almost like I was "coming home" to a version of myself that I had put in the dark once I got to college.

***

When I did my student teaching, I felt that my students respected me for the most part. In the United States, teachers usually do not receive the respect they deserve for an extensive list of reasons that I am going to spare you the time for until Chapter 17. Once I open that can of worms, I'll be writing a manifesto instead of a memoir; but ultimately, it comes down to how our society undervalues education. They told us in college that students don't always respect younger teachers, especially because they think they can push boundaries and get away with more (speaking from experience, there is some truth in that.).

One experience from my student teaching that has stuck with me was from a day in the 10th grade German class I had recently started teaching. With this class specifically, it was the last class that I took over, so I didn't have as much time to build a connection with the students as their teacher. One day in class, I had planned for us to play Bingo to practice the vocabulary we just learned. We had about ten minutes left of class, and when I began passing out the Bingo cards, a couple students said they didn't want to play, and several others joined in this sentiment. It snowballed quickly into many of them saying that they weren't going to play, and eventually, the majority of the class decided to band together.

My mentor teacher was not in the room at the time, so I knew I had to regain control on my own. I expressed to them that I had worked hard to plan my lesson, but I wasn't upset that they didn't think this part of it would be fun. I was upset because I felt that their behavior was disrespectful, and they weren't seeing how much work I was putting into being there. I was working the same hours and doing the same work that a full-time teacher would, along with studying for and completing my licensure exams and graduation requirements. On top of that, I wasn't being paid for any of my work. I wasn't just there because I had to be; I was there because I genuinely wanted to be. I wanted to do something fun with them, because learning a language can be heavily grammar-focused and kind of boring, so I thought playing Bingo would be a nice break at the end of class. I told them how it made me feel, especially considering how much of my time I spent preparing for each day. The class ended, and the students left in silence.

The universe has an interesting way of working things out, because in the class of 9th graders that followed, it was one student's birthday, and they had brought a cake in to share with the class. I knew immediately when they asked if we could celebrate at the end of the lesson that I needed to take a moment to release my emotions from what happened in the class before. It would not be fair for me to bring that same energy into the next class. I, of course, said that we could celebrate, and I thanked the students who asked for brightening my mood when I truly needed it. I think some of the students had heard me talking to the previous class

CHAPTER SIXTEEN

before they came in, because that day, it was the smoothest class ever. We had fun spending the last ten minutes eating cake and singing Happy Birthday—talk about polar opposite differences between the end of both classes.

After school, a few students from the 10th grade class came into the room and apologized for how everyone behaved, and I appreciated hearing that from them, even if they were not the ones who were being rude. I spoke with my mentor teacher about how to go about handling the 10th grade class the next day. She suggested ideas, but ultimately, she left the decision up to me.

As I was reflecting on the day as I drove back to campus, I thought about how the students behaved. *What could have prompted that behavior or made them think it was okay to be so hurtful?* I realized that one possibility was that they did not feel any type of real connection to me, because we hadn't had as much time together. This was understandable to me, because I believe in the power of the student-teacher relationship and that in order for students to truly learn, they have to feel connected to what they are learning about and who they are learning from. After having this realization, I began planning for class the next day.

While I believe teaching the class content is important—that's obviously the reason why we are all there—, I felt that it was important for me to dedicate time to allowing the students to get to know me better and vice versa. To accomplish this, I decided that for class the next day, I would offer the students two journal prompts. To foster language in the classroom, I provided them the prompts in German and gave them the option to write in English or German. For the majority of the class, I spent time explaining my answers to both journal prompts with pictures and stories from my life. Here were the two journal prompts I gave to the students, but for them, the prompts were in German:

1. Who is a person that you respect? Why do you respect them? Describe this person and their role in your life.
2. What is a mistake you have made in your life? Why was it a mistake? What did you learn from this experience?

For the first prompt, I told the students about my friend Jade. I described to them how we met during the first weekend of college, and how she has been one of the kindest, most unique, and amazing people I have ever met in my life. I talked about how she had been there for me throughout some of the darkest moments in my life, never judging me, and always believing in my strength. She is more than a friend; she is a soulmate; she is part of my family.

I also talked about my sister Nina and how I respect her confidence. When we were little, we were in a four-wheeling accident, and she lost her front tooth. That experience, I believe, is one of the pillars of her confidence, because from an early age, she had to overcome the insecurity of missing one of her "permanent" teeth. She used to joke that she lost it while playing hockey, and that definitely intimidated the other teams she played against.

For the second prompt, I told them about the car accident I was in with my sister Sabrina. I was their age when it happened, and I describe how it made me feel because of my eye disorder. I shared what I learned from this experience with them, and I encouraged them to never take anything for granted, especially those they call their family.

CHAPTER SIXTEEN

For the last fifteen minutes of class, the students had time to write their own responses and share stories from their own personal experiences. When I tell you these kids were so invested in what I was saying, and that I had never heard a quieter class that you could tell were paying attention, I truly mean it. When they had time to write about their own experiences, every single one of them spent a majority of that time writing. Some students sloughed it off and only wrote a couple sentences, but that was only two or three. At the end of class, they handed these responses in, and I told them that I would respond to every single one of them in writing. Several more students apologized for their behavior the day before and thanked me for being vulnerable with them.

This is probably one of my favorite memories from my student teaching, because from that day forward, there were never any issues with this class. I could feel that they not only respected me but valued my presence in the classroom. I will always have a special place in my heart for those kids, not only in that specific class, but all the kids I taught during those few months before the pandemic turned our world upside down.

***

When I had to leave the school due to the COVID-19 pandemic, it was surreal. I remember my college emailing us on Friday, March 13 about how the campus would be closing and we had to go home. That next Monday, I stood next to my mentor teacher and talked to those high school kids about what the next couple of weeks would look like. I remember sitting there looking at those kids, knowing that their world—our world—would never be the same after those moments. How do you tell someone that? That their entire world is going to not only change, but probably never be the same again.

Those last few days I spent with my college friends were some of the most emotional I've experienced. We went from thinking that we had a couple months before graduation to only having a couple days or hours to see our friends before saying goodbye for who knew how long. So many tears were shed. Many of those people were family; we kept each other sane. They genuinely knew *me*, in ways that my friends back home and blood-relatives did not. It felt like my closest allies were being ripped away from me. Almost two years later, and there are still some people I haven't seen since.

It was a difficult and uncertain time. That being said, when this was all happening, I had quite a different perspective about the potential outcome. I felt this would be a time of growth, destruction, and hopefully rebirth for our society. I knew that as the world and the aspects of my ego crumbled around me, in the end, I would make it out a different version of myself.

The next few months after the start of the pandemic would also allow me the space to look at societal conditioning from as objective of a viewpoint as possible, trying not to victimize or blame it, but simply observe it. Living in a society isn't all bad, but the pressure and the judgment to be a certain way is overwhelming. I often question if I want to live in this society because sometimes it blows my mind how much it sucks, especially after seeing all of the injustice that occurs within many of its systems such as the education, criminal justice, and healthcare system. But then I think of the people I have met in this society, the possible opportunities to experience, and the ability to travel to beautiful places on the planet. This is all possible because of a "society" and how it interacts with others around the globe.

For the longest time, it was difficult for me to express my

CHAPTER SIXTEEN

thoughts and feelings about this time period in words. I struggled to convey the meaning I perceived and interpreted in my head to the outside world. In previous situations where I struggled to articulate my thoughts, this often led to feeling misunderstood by others, frustrated with myself, and honestly confused about why it was so difficult.

The thoughts and feelings I experienced at the start of the pandemic were not necessarily unique to me—every human being is capable of feeling these same feelings, thinking these same thoughts—so why was it so hard for me to articulate them? It all stems back to feeling like I couldn't express myself as a child. Considering the amount of growth and change I have experienced since then, but especially over the last few years, I think it's safe to say that my body needed rest and time to truly reflect on how the experiences in my past still influenced me.

I would compare this time period, from the start of the pandemic up until when I am writing this now, to the process of the caterpillar turning into a butterfly that I mentioned in a previous chapter. When we look at a butterfly, we're in amazement at the transformation and how beautiful the butterfly is, but we don't think much about the discomfort of that transformation. Think about it, while a caterpillar is in a cocoon, it is literally changing into a whole different thing. If I were a butterfly, I could imagine that that's gotta be uncomfortable; and there would probably be a point where I'd be confused and would question what the hell is going on as one wing starts to develop and then the other. When you are in your late teens and twenties, you are the caterpillar in the cocoon. You are having your own metamorphosis, going from your own version of the caterpillar to a butterfly. That transformation doesn't happen overnight, and it probably won't be very easy. And when the butterfly starts to break the shell and emerge from the cocoon, it will probably hurt or be uncomfortable. But give it time, that butterfly is coming out of the cocoon when she feels she's ready to share her beauty with the world.

Questions to Contemplate:

1. **Who is a person that I respect? Why do I respect them? Describe this person and their role in my life.**
2. **What is a mistake I have made in my life? Why was it a mistake? What did I learn from this experience?**
3. **How did I feel when I realized how seriously the pandemic would affect our world?**

V

METAMORPHOSIS

17

CHAPTER SEVENTEEN

Something that happens in your twenties that not many people talk about is that all of a sudden, you feel like you don't know who you are and that you have no friends. It can feel incredibly lonely. But the thing is, when you're a kid, your standards for who your friends are and who you spend your time with are pretty low and circumstantial. At that time in your life, your main ambition is to finish school, pretty simple. But as you get older, you refine your standards and learn how to set healthy boundaries. It is totally natural for you to grieve the loss of certain friendships because it feels like you're losing a part of yourself, an innocence that no longer exists. Allow yourself to grieve the loss of those people in your life who, at one point, may have been your entire world, but now, no longer align with your growth. You can still maintain the quality of the *memories* you had with those people, without holding onto the *people* themselves. Your twenties, at least so far in my experience, are basically one big time period of identity crisis that each person moves through at a different rate.

After graduating college in 2020, it was not long after that I began to have a bit of an identity crisis myself. I would say this is something that every college graduate faces, but when you are graduating in the midst of a pandemic, it feels weird. Part of me was relieved to be experiencing it during a pandemic because when people asked me what I wanted to do with my life now, it was not abnormal for me to say that I had no clue; and they couldn't judge me for it because at the time, no one knew what the future would be like because of the virus.

When I graduated, I moved back home because it made the most sense financially, and considering what was going on in the world, a little stability couldn't hurt. This time period gave me the opportunity to consider what I wanted to do next. The thing is, I could do anything, literally anything. That is a powerful feeling, but it can also be extremely overwhelming to have so many possibilities, especially if there are other circumstances to consider like paying rent, feeding your family, health concerns, etc. It is also terrifying because you don't want to pick the "wrong" one. I didn't know which direction I wanted to go in. (Side note, I don't really believe there is a "wrong" choice you can make. The universe works in mysterious ways, and all comes to fruition in divine timing.) For the longest time, I have had something to guide me in a direction. I was in school for thirteen years before graduating high school; then I was in college for four years. It was a logical progression that society had imposed on me, and it was a path that I felt made the most sense. But once I made it to the end of that path, I didn't know which direction I wanted to go from there.

There were definitely times when I didn't want to get out of bed, and I didn't know if there was something wrong with me, or if I just wanted to have a lazy day. I didn't necessarily want to be alone, but I also didn't always want to be around other people. In those moments, I would sometimes get out of bed and go for a walk around my neighborhood. Looking at the world around me and being aware of my surroundings in the moment allowed me to recharge my batteries without feeling like I needed to be "productive." "Productivity culture" can be overly obsessive with outcomes and results rather than trusting the process and taking your time. Listening to music was also very therapeutic for me and inspired me to be creative in new ways. I fell back in love with painting and expressing myself through art. I also began reading books for fun again. The thing is low moments are inevitable. The most important thing you can do for yourself in those moments is to give yourself grace and allow yourself to rest, because you will experience a high point again.

***

Before the pandemic, I applied to be an English Teaching Assistant through the Fulbright Program. The Fulbright Program is considered one of the largest educational and cultural exchange programs. It is sponsored by the U.S. government, and its goal is to foster mutual understanding between the people and cultures of the United States with those of other countries around the world. I had been selected to teach in Germany during the 2020-21 school year. However, because of the state of the pandemic at the time, my program was initially delayed and then eventually postponed until the next school year.

In the meantime, my German teacher from high school was having a baby, and because I now had a license to teach German, she asked if I would be her long-term substitute while she was on maternity leave. So, for the first month of the 2020-21 school year, I was back teaching at the high school I graduated from. After completing that month, I was offered a more permanent position as a substitute teacher at the middle school for the rest of the year. I decided that, because initial plans were postponed, this could be a great learning opportunity for me during my first official year of teaching. And boy, was I right. Being a teacher during the COVID-19 pandemic was quite the experience but being a *first-year* teacher and working as a substitute on top of that added a whole other layer to my learning curve.

It was interesting for me to be back in my hometown and teaching alongside people who that were once my teachers. It felt like I was coming full circle, back to where it all started. Many of these teachers were role models to me when I was a kid, but I also learned from them as colleagues and mentors during that year, not only in terms of teaching, but also life skills in general. They inspired many of the following thoughts on my perspective of life as a young adult in the 21st century.

***

One day, I was sitting in the teacher's lounge eating lunch with about five or six other teachers. One of them was talking about what her son has been up to since finishing his first semester of his senior year at college. She said that he was taking off a semester because of COVID and will finish his degree in the fall. He hadn't found a job to work in the meantime or really shown much interest or progress with looking for a one. On the other hand, her daughter is a couple years younger, and she had been making connections and networking within a major and career field that she was interested in but hadn't yet committed to. Her son was

CHAPTER SEVENTEEN

about 21, and her daughter was about 19. Another teacher mentioned the point that "kids that age think they have it figured out, but they don't." *Why do they believe that? What gives them this impression? How was their experience different?* As I was looking around the room, gauging the reactions of the others, I made eye contact with another teacher in the room who was also in her twenties. Many of the others, who were around the same age as or a little bit older than the one sharing the story, agreed with that statement. They began talking about what writing a resume was like when they were that age and the process of looking for jobs. They suggested things that her son could be doing right now or resources he could be taking advantage of to do more for his potential career path.

This situation provoked some thoughts within me about the topic of this conversation because they weren't completely wrong. I can only speak from my experience, but I know I am not alone in this sentiment. "Kids my age" try to *pretend* we have it figured out because that is what society has told us we need to do. But the truth is, we are well-aware that we have absolutely no idea what is going on sometimes. However, I feel that there is a difference in perspective and awareness between people around my age, the same age as that of this teacher's kids, and those who were born in an earlier generation. Given the fact that there was a substantial difference in the actions of her son and daughter (which I have also generally observed within my peers), one could probably also make a case about the differences between the male and female perspective cognitively, but for the sake of this chapter, I am going to discuss them collectively as a generational difference rather than based on a biological, developmental, or socially constructed difference.

I will not claim to speak for everyone in my generation, so when I use the words "we" or "us," I am referencing my *perception* of my generation. I feel that we are becoming more aware of the state of our society as we get older. Duh, obviously, that is part of growing up. But I feel that we, as a society, are becoming more conscious in multiple areas; and with that, comes an evolved species—each generation "better off" than the next. With the implementation and continual development of modern technologies, we, by consequence, are being asked to evolve at a faster rate—or at least, it feels like it. What I'm trying to say is that I feel like the level of consciousness I have at the age of 22, and the level of consciousness my generation has overall is higher than that of where our parents and grandparents were at our age. We are becoming more aware of our impact on the world and the impact of the role we play or do not play in this society.

We have realized that the current purpose of our school system is not education. Unfortunately, our schools are serving the same functions as factories, prisons, and mental institutions by attempting to define, classify, control, and regulate desired behavioral outcomes. It is common for a student to ask a question about *why* something is the way that it is within our system or society, and to have it be met with resistance or dismissal. But we have to be asking these questions. I believe that the most important form of a question you can ask is, "Why?"

Why? Questioning your reality and your identity are normal parts of the human experience. Some of the questions my generation is contemplating are, "Why do we work a 9-5, and why is it so normalized to put in so much labor for a company that probably doesn't value your health or well-being over their profit margin?"; "Why do we work jobs we hate where we are counting down the hours until we're done in order to pay for things we are told we need?"; "Why do so many people feel the need to numb themselves with the consumption of senseless content?"; "Why are we continuing to destroy our planet and alienate ourselves from the natural world when this planet is our home and what gives us life?"; and "How does all of this nonsense that we are conditioned to believe and think is normal in schools influence how we feel about learning and making mistakes?"

From my perspective, it is not that I believe I have life figured out or that I know better than others. I *know* that I don't know what I'm doing a lot of the time. Many young people know this about themselves as well; we are aware of this, and we have to be okay with it, to an extent. I have an understanding that I have no clue how to *do* life or what *life* necessarily means. But the thing is, I don't want to *do* life; I want to *live* life. In response to that teacher's comment about "kids that age" thinking they have it all figured out, I respect your perspective, but we do not think we know everything—we feel quite the contrary, I'd say. It may come across that way, because many of us are scared of failure and really good at masking our emotions. The flip side of that is many of us are so passionate about what we feel, especially if we are witnessing injustice, that we'll say what's on our minds whether we know better or not.

The truth of the matter is, many of us feel lost. We feel blatantly disregarded, ignored, and misunderstood within a system that doesn't align with our values and beliefs for a greater future. And we don't know how to cope with that when no one seems to be listening.

There are so many systems in our country that do not work, and too many people who believe that there is nothing wrong with them. We cannot simply hope and pray that things get better. At this moment, I feel that the society in the United States is eventually doomed to more division, violence, and unrest unless something changes. It is no secret that the education system is not adequately preparing our youth for the very real problems that they will face. When do we finally decide that enough is enough and that we cannot keep repeating this cycle with how we raise and "educate" our kids? I feel like many have realized that, but others continue to perpetuate the cycle out of fear for the unknown.

Being a teacher is demanding work, and to work in a system that creates so much inequality and injustice, a system that does not respect you and gives you less than the bare minimum, is frustrating. I would go so far as to claim that our society in the United States does not value education as a fundamental tool to freedom. That is demonstrated in a multitude of ways such as the whitewashing of history curriculum, average salary of a public school teacher, the lack of representation in decision making processes for grade standards, overall public opinion, and so on. This system frustrates me to no foreseeable end, but I know education is power. It is what allows one to rise above ignorance. It is a pathway to freedom. And while this system may frustrate me, I believe that we have the knowledge and ability to create a better one.

***

Our society has told us that if we follow all of the correct steps, we will be successful and happy. But let me tell you, I followed the steps, I was a great student, I graduated college, I got a decent job, but none of that on its own made me feel like

CHAPTER SEVENTEEN

I could be successful or happy.

So, if you are not sure what you want to do after graduating high school, and you don't know what type of career you're interested in going into, do not, I repeat, DO NOT put yourself into an enormous amount of debt in order to go to college. The internet is free, and there are so many resources online that can help you make a wiser decision for far less money. And as a little reminder, it is also completely okay to change your mind about a job or career that you pursue, no matter how far along you get with it. You have time.

I knew I wanted to pursue a career in education, whether that meant working in the public school system or another area of education. That being said, in order to finance my goals and dreams, I knew that I would have to learn how to make my money work for me by creating multiple streams of income, besides the paycheck I would be working for. Those are two of the biggest lessons I learned while becoming financially literate: make your money work for you and create multiple streams of income.

For most of my life, my relationship with money was not a healthy one. Seeing how my parents managed their money and the struggles they faced because of their finances, along with the experiences I had with money while living in Austria, made me view money in a negative way. For years, I complained about how stupid it is that our school system doesn't teach us about money and how it works in our society. Going into 2020, one of my goals was to become financially literate and take my finances into my own hands. The pandemic provided the perfect opportunity to do this because there came a point when I decided that I was fed up with not knowing how money worked. I was done complaining about my situation, so I began learning more.

Throughout several months of being at home during the pandemic, I watched YouTube videos, listened to podcasts, followed many business and finance creators on TikTok, and read self-help books to learn about the basics of money. I opened my first credit card to consciously build my credit score, started an investment account for retirement, and slowly separated myself from my parents' finances. While it has only been a little over a year since I started this educational journey, I already believe that this was one of the best decisions I've made for myself. I believe that it has transformed the way I now view my relationship with money. I am confident that as I continue learning and putting what I have learned into practice, I will be able to accomplish so many things that I once did not know how I would make happen.

If there was one thing that I think all young adults should do after they graduate high school or college, it would be to learn about money and become financially literate. It is an absolute necessity in our society; and even though I despise how much money dictates our society, that does not change the truth of it. If one does not understand the power of money and how to use it, then they will become subjected to its power rather than in control of it. Money is a form of energy in the sense that as it is transferred from one person to another and, it can create and take away power. Another lesson I learned from improving my financial literacy is this: if you don't know how to do something, don't settle for your own excuses, teach yourself.

Questions to Contemplate:

CHAPTER SEVENTEEN

1. **What drains my energy? What gives me energy?**
2. **What motivates me (money, curiosity, fear, happiness, etc.)?**
3. **What do I want less of in my life? What do I want more of? Why?**

CHAPTER EIGHTEEN

Moving back home during the pandemic came with being thrust back into the family dynamics that I hadn't lived in for an extensive amount of time since I was in high school. For the first few months, it was hard for me to adjust to living with my family again. One of my younger sisters had moved into my room after I left for college, so I was also in the process of turning our basement living room into my own space. I feel like a lot of college graduates and young adults who move back in with their parents can relate to this. Even if you're moving back into the same room you lived in when you were a child, there is definitely a difference in family dynamics and how you feel being back in that space. Apart from making my new physical space a home that would support the newest version of myself, I was also maneuvering through creating healthy habits and focusing on my relationship with my mental health.

I have found that there are varying opinions surrounding the efficacy of therapy versus self-help, and I believe that it varies for each person and each situation. Since Because therapy was not an accessible option for me personally at this time, I realized that I would have to outline a plan for myself to heal from those wounds. While this wasn't necessarily a document or physical "plan" at the beginning, I started with writing down a list of the most important memories I could remember. I also used several journal prompts to write about these experiences and new ones that I hadn't thought of before. Once I began writing and patiently moving through these memories, I quickly learned that it is difficult to heal in the environment that made you sick.

Living at home, I had time to come back to my roots. That meant taking into account not only the roots that were healthy and bringing in nutrients to feed my soul, but also the roots that were broken off or diseased and taking nutrients away. When I stumbled upon a new root that wasn't sustaining me anymore, I acknowledged its impact on me by feeling and releasing the emotions I had kept buried under the surface for so long. One by one, taking my time, I was shining a light on the shadows I had been hiding from. Slowly, but surely, those shadows became smaller, and some even disappeared over time. But don't let the poetic wording fool you; this was at times exceedingly difficult and emotionally painful to do on my own, and sometimes, the best way to let a wound heal is to stop constantly touching it.

When it comes to childhood trauma and maneuvering through an evolving relationship with your parents, I learned that you could love your parents while also acknowledging and accepting that they may not have provided for all of your needs, including your emotional ones, when you were a child. I feel that we need to reject this idea that our parents have to be perfect examples, especially when many of them struggle with their own undiagnosed childhood trauma. Parenting is not always black and white—I'm not a parent, but I would bet that there is absolutely some grey area when it comes to the best way to raise kids. However, it is important to consider how you were raised in the context of how your parents were raised. When it comes to evaluating your childhood and its effect on you and your relationship with them as an adult, it is completely okay for you to take the space you need. There are things that cannot be excused, and this is where forgiveness is easier said than done, because it is your decision whether to forgive your parents for making mistakes. There is a difference between making a mistake and actively inflicting harm. As an adult, you are now the one to decide how large or small of a role your parents will continue to play in your life.

***

Existentialism, exploring the human experience through philosophical inquiry, is something that I spend a great deal of my time contemplating. At times, I would say that I spend an unhealthy amount of time thinking about the problems and consequences of the human experience; it baffles me and hurts my heart to think about the monstrous things humans are capable of. Let's just say, these thought patterns are a weekly occurrence in my mind, and that is where therapy would probably be more beneficial for me than trying to work through those thoughts and feelings on my own.

It is easy to spiral into cynicism. While I believe it is important to be aware of what is going on in the world, it is not healthy to obsess over everything that happens. Human beings were not meant to be aware of every single tragedy that occurs all the time, but the internet has made that possible and easily accessible, and I can't forget to mention the dopamine addictions that make it hard to look away from our screens. During the early months of the pandemic, this was especially true. Personally, being aware of the disparities and injustices that were occurring was a source of immense stress and sadness that I wasn't prepared to handle. I often cried myself to sleep out of frustration.

That being said, I feel that the world doesn't necessarily need more optimists either, but rather, more people who are aware of themselves. People who are aware of their emotions, their mistakes, their goals, their passions, their complexity. But most importantly, I feel that we need more people who are aware of their humanity *and* the humanity of others.

I think the beautiful thing about growing older is becoming conscious of the potential life has. When we are kids, we don't always see beyond the age that we are. The "future" is a weird concept for us to understand in terms of "growing up." As you become aware of "growing up" or of "life" itself, your perspective on how you live changes. At least, that's what happened to me. As I matured throughout college and continued to challenge and push myself intellectually, I began to understand that our purpose in life is to experience it. The meaning of life is what we perceive it to be. Ultimately, maybe there is some greater purpose to life, and maybe there's not. All I know is that one day, my time will come, and my soul will leave this body. So, until then, I am doing my best to make the most of each moment, *in the moment*, to spread the light I have to those I encounter.

***

It's time for me to introduce you to a woman named Kari. She was basically like another grandma or aunt for me—everyone in my family referred to her as "Aunt Kari."

Her and her husband were remarkably close to my grandma and grandpa (my dad's parents) for decades. They lived in Nebraska while my grandparents lived in South Dakota, but they would come to visit my grandparents' house when we had family get-togethers, and they even spent some family vacations with us. Long story short, they were family.

For a while, our family would spend about a week at a cabin resort on a lake in Minnesota each summer. We would spend the week fishing, tubing, having bonfires, and partying it up with the family. My family on my dad's side is pretty big, and my sisters and I are on the younger side of the twenty-two cousins, so I didn't always feel close to them.

I have one very distinct memory from when I was little. My mom, a couple of my aunts, my grandma, Aunt Kari, and I were playing bocce ball behind the cabins by the rest of the campground and the playground. When we were choosing partners, I chose Aunt Kari because I was pretty young, and she seemed like a nice, safe lady. She was a teacher throughout her entire career; and when I think about that memory now, it is obvious to me that she worked with kids because the way she could strike up and continue any conversation with me at that age was what made me feel safe and comfortable around her.

As I've said, I was quiet growing up, and I didn't always talk much at large family gatherings. With that many people, someone else was usually dominating the conversation. I was also one of the youngest ones, so most of my cousins were older. They had grown up around one another because most of them still lived in South Dakota (my dad and one of his sisters had moved to Minnesota long before I was born). Aunt Kari made me feel more included in my family whenever she was around than most of my actual family members did because she actually talked to me. Even as I got older and her grandchildren came to South Dakota to visit, she would always strike up a conversation with me about whatever I was up to.

In the spring of 2021, she passed away. At this point, her husband and my grandpa had preceded her in death, so when she passed away, my grandma was the only one left of the four. I was in the process of writing this book and hadn't even considered including her influence on my life. But when she passed away, it brought up so many emotions. That was when I realized just how significant of a role this woman had played in my life. I may not have known her entire life story, but the handful of times I was with her had the most profound, wonderful impact on my life, redefining what it means to be "family." And for that, I thank her.

Before her funeral, my grandma talked about the last time Kari called her on the phone and how it felt like she was saying goodbye. "Goodbyes" are something you should never take for granted because you truly never know when it will be the last time you see someone. I imagine it feels quite different when you know it is probably the last time you'll talk to a friend you've known for over 50 years. How do you say goodbye to someone you've known for the majority of your life? How do you feel and process that? I haven't even been on this planet for a quarter of a century yet, let alone spent my life with someone for twice that amount of time.

How does your perspective on death change when you lose someone like that? When you are young, it feels like there is a sense of invincibility to death. Taking risks in your teenage years and your twenties is a lot easier because *death* doesn't necessarily feel as real or tangible. It is something that affects us all differently, but it affects us all nonetheless because no one is immune to it.

In my generation, many of us feel apathetic towards death. We grew up in a post-9/11, post-Columbine world, where terrorist attacks and school shootings were normalized in our media and society. We have been trained how to fend for our lives since Kindergarten, for crying out loud. On top of that, mental illness and the climate crisis have led to many feeling unfazed and even numb to the idea of death. and I wonder what the long-term impact of that will be.? When we are the ones who are old and dying, will our collective perspective as a generation change?

***

Death is not the greatest loss of life. The greatest loss of life is what dies inside of us as we grow older.

We are told when we are younger to follow our dreams and use our imagination. I can remember a day in 1st grade when we were supposed to dress up as what we wanted to be when we were older. I dressed up as a teacher—hey, look at me now with two different teaching licenses. From an early age, I listened to the whispers of my soul when it told me to pursue a career in education. However, I can confidently tell you today that while I am extremely enthusiastic about education and the power it has, I will not be working as a public school teacher for long. There are so many issues within our education system that make it morally impossible for me to commit myself to it for 10+ years. Besides that, there is great inequality when it comes to education in our world, and I believe that my voice can be more useful where it is valued.

It is truly a shame that so many people give up on their dreams from when they were children. Today, I am writing this specific passage while sitting on a park bench in Freiburg im Breisgau, Germany. At one time in my life, being here was nothing but a dream, a goal, a hope. Before moving here, many people told me that they were excited for me to follow my dreams. They said that they were jealous of the opportunities I would have here. I believe that their jealousy was not purely in vain or an expression of envy for my situation, but a mourning of what they once dreamed they could do. Many people give up on their dreams or do not believe them to be possible; and that, in my opinion, is the greatest loss of life.

You can look at life in several ways. To simplify, you can look at it and think, "What's the point? There's no point in doing anything. How can I win?" Or you can look at life and think, "I don't know what the point is, or if there even is one, BUT isn't that in itself kinda the point? There's no losing as long as I can sustain my basic needs, do things that bring me joy, and surround myself with some kickass people I love." It is all about how you choose to perceive it. There is, of course, a privilege that comes along with how you are able to attain that freedom, but the world is literally your blank canvas, waiting for you to create your masterpiece. I believe it is important to express the gratitude I have for the privileges and opportunities I receive in this life, because I feel it is my responsibility to use them to help uplift others as well.

Questions to Contemplate:

1. **If I died tomorrow, would I be satisfied with the life I've lived? Why?**
2. **What emotions have I avoided feeling in the past? Why? What do I need to let go of or release?**

3. **How often do I say, "I love you"? How do I express my appreciation and love for others? How often?**

CHAPTER NINETEEN

Most of 2020 felt like walking through a thick fog. I didn't exactly know where I was going, but I had to trust my instincts and allow my intuition to guide me through. At first, I didn't even know where I was looking, but slowly the fog started to clear when I took a step back, and objectively looked at how I got to where I was. It wasn't a straightforward process, and at times it was hard to find a purpose in continuing to move forward in a world where it is so easy to feel defeated. That being said, I understand what it's like to not feel in control, what it feels like to be lost and confused. In the grand scheme of my life, 22 years could be a relatively short time; and in the grand scheme of the universe, that is almost no time at all.

I have heard many people refer to your twenties as the best years of your life. While that may have been true for them, personally, this is my primer, my warm-up, if you will. I want to make the most of the time I have on this planet because it is never guaranteed. There are going to be so many more mistakes that I'll make, but rather than giving in and choosing the easy path, I am deciding to take control of my life and radically accept all that comes with it. I have learned that there truly is no inherent meaning to life. It is all about the meaning and perspective that you give it. My purpose in this life is to simply *live*. That's it. I could describe a higher purpose for myself that includes the goals and aspirations that I have for my personal and professional life, but those are not my true "purpose"—and they're not yours either. Goals and dreams are a wonderful guide on your journey, but they do not dictate the path. There's nothing you *need* to accomplish in this lifetime, so you are in control of when your journey changes direction.

Self-awareness also comes into play here when setting goals for yourself, both big and small. With the endless refresh cycle of social media, it's easy to get lost in the accomplishments and "success" of other people. Speaking from experience, passion and authenticity are lost when comparison is thrown into the mix. One of the many dangers of social media is that with every second you spend consuming content and scrolling on your phone, your mind is producing opinions and judgments rather than forming original thoughts. Many of the ideas and opinions produced are not necessarily your own; your brain would probably not have wandered or came to that conclusion if you weren't influenced by looking at content on a screen.

This doesn't always have to be interpreted as a negative thing. One can learn a great deal from the world of social media by connecting with humans from all walks of life. That is incredible, and there is immense power in that. For me personally, it externally validated that I was hurt and that I deserved to heal from the wounds of my past. Connecting with others online can help you recognize how the world can be unfair and contradictory. Knowing that, it is important to take a step back and consider which ideas and opinions are actually your own and which ones were put there by someone else. After all, we ought to authentically express ourselves. Many societies try to dictate this, but ultimately, it is our choice. Grounding yourself in nature or simply being present in the physical world around you will allow you to become more aware of your thought patterns.

There is this concept called confirmation bias where one is consciously or unconsciously looking for information to confirm what they have been told or believe. When it comes to misinformation, we have seen how detrimental this can be within a society. Likewise, it can also be detrimental to yourself. If you are telling yourself that you are a shitty person and nothing ever works out for you and you don't deserve love and happiness, then your brain is going to focus on everything in your life that confirms those beliefs. When you become aware of these thought patterns and begin to change your thoughts, your brain will begin to focus on the things that reinforce those new beliefs. Even simply asking yourself or a higher power, "How can I change? How can this get any better?" will create a new connection in your brain, where it begins looking for evidence of, and inspiration to, make real change in your life. The beautiful thing is, the more you practice this awareness, the more you begin to see.

This doesn't have to be something rooted in negativity either. I mentioned that confirmation bias in a world of misinformation can be detrimental. Setting the intention of self-growth and becoming more self-aware is crucial without getting lost in what some may call "toxic positivity." It isn't about being egotistical, in fact your ego will fight you on changing your thought patterns, or about thinking that you are better than anyone else. It is about realizing your own personal power and capability of creating your own reality. I felt lost in the fog for a while because after having a spiritual awakening a couple years prior, I knew that I was capable and deserving of happiness, but I didn't know what the next step on my journey was. I realized that that feeling of being lost, stuck, or simply not knowing what to do with my time was an important transition for me. The biggest changes in my mindset came during those moments of sitting with my thoughts and healing my inner child. When I began creating change in my life and turning my dreams into a reality, there were many people who saw this and became jealous.

There may be people in your life who root for you to your face or on the surface, but deep down, they resent your confidence and self-assurance. It is frustrating to see yourself making progress and then hear from people who you thought would support you that they don't believe in what you're doing. Let me let you in on a little secret; most of the time, when people tell you that you cannot do something or that something will be impossible to achieve, they are projecting their own insecurities, regret, disbelief, and lack of self-confidence onto you.

Remember that while other people's opinions and advice may provide some sense of guidance, you have the ability to guide yourself. Everything you need to change your mindset is already within you. You are here to live and *experience* this life. When you begin to radically accept *everything* that happens in your life—my personal favorite motto is "It is what it is"—you can accomplish anything you set your mind to.

Radical acceptance is a concept that I have been practicing for the past couple years, but I didn't always have the words to label or describe it. *Pain* is a natural part of life, but practicing radical acceptance has allowed me to prevent it turning into *suffering*. Writing this book has been an act of radical acceptance. It required me to look at some of the most amazing and happiest memories in my life until this point while also looking at some of my saddest and most embarrassing memories. I cannot change the facts of these events, nor do I have to approve of or be apathetic towards them. *I accept them for what they are.* Instead of fighting reality or responding with impulsive or destructive behaviors, I accept that I cannot change what happened, and I now understand the circumstances that caused those events. This understanding allows me to control the power they continue to have over me. This practice has released me from remaining stuck in those feelings of jealousy, resentment, and anger that were causing me to suffer internally as a child.

I've heard people say that you should spend your early twenties alone. I understand and agree with where the sentiment comes from, but I also respect that for some people, they fall in love with themselves as they fall in love with another. Love is a topic that I am fascinated with learning and talking about, but most importantly, experiencing. For me, I have found that I feel the most love and give the most love to people around me when I have taken care of myself fully and set that intention with myself as a priority. There are so many possibilities for how we choose to live this life. For many, that fact alone is extremely daunting and scary, which is completely valid because, oh my gosh, the possibilities are endless. For me personally, I know being on my own is what is best for me at this point of my life. In your early twenties, you are learning to understand what you value and what fulfills you. At this stage, what's the hurry?

I am choosing to break the cycle and conditioning that has been ingrained in me since birth. This is not the time where I am choosing the practical and safe route of getting the job, the car, the house, the partner, etc. that everyone expects of me. At this point, my priority is to maximize my happiness rather than any amount of money or material wealth because all of that means nothing if you aren't happy with your life or the choices you've made. Making this choice means concretely exploring my values and what piques my interest. My approach may be more risk-oriented, but I recognize how lucky I am to be living this life, in the world we are in today.

***

Death is something that a lot of people are afraid of, but in my opinion, death itself is not what they fear. The fear lies in living a life, looking back on it, and realizing that they didn't live at all. It's not about leaving an impression or being remembered, but rather, feeling that their life had meaning. Many people don't want to leave this life without knowing that they're happy with how they lived it. So, if you've been waiting for a sign to make that first leap, this is your sign to give your dreams a chance. If you fail, change your course of action, and try again. The thing about dreams is, they never give up on you; it usually happens the other way around.

Pursuing your dreams can be a scary and daunting journey, but I would encourage you to do things that scare you. If you make a decision and you are afraid of failure being the outcome, that's how you know you made the right one. Your ego will do everything in its power to protect you, that's its job. Sometimes, that is at the cost of your own success—thanks, ego. It may be your biggest enemy, because the thoughts your ego tells you have been programmed by society and your surroundings. Progress and growth happen when you step outside of your comfort zone. I know that's cliche, but it's the truth. When you are becoming an adult, one of your biggest challenges is going to be tuning out the expectations and opinions of others. Listen to your heart, pay attention to what excites you, and become aware of how your thoughts influence your emotions.

There is a very real possibility that taking that leap of faith will work out way better than what you were anticipating. Because your ego is trying to protect you from the worst possible outcome, it closes your eyes to the best possible outcome. Being an overthinker and working through perfectionism, my mind is a professional at this point in thinking of the worst possible situation for almost anything. However, in my experience, while being prepared for those outcomes is sometimes helpful, they rarely ever actually happen.

There have been so many experiences in my life where I wanted to give up or back down. In those moments when it was hard for me to believe in myself, I believed that eventually it would all work out in the end. If I had already made it that far and things hadn't worked themselves out yet, then it wasn't the end, and I kept going. Looking back on those experiences, most of them worked out far better than I could have even imagined at the time. That may not be the case for every situation, but more often than not, you'd be surprised by with what you are capable of accomplishing when you learn to understand and move through your own fears.

Time for some tough love. I can sit here, and tell you that you are the most important person in your life. I can tell you over and over again that falling in love with life is the key to happiness. I can share my own stories and experiences of how I got here and what I learned along the way. But the truth is, at the end of the day, long story short, you have to believe it for yourself. Your happiness is your responsibility. Whether you believe you can live a happy life or not, you are correct. Believing in yourself is being self-aware that you are capable. Visualize what your idea of happiness looks like and how you would get there. You would not have made it to the end of this book if you did not believe you could. In the last chapter, I write about how gratitude is what led me here today. But right now, I want to say thank you, wherever you are on your journey, for reading this far. We are creating the reality of our world together.

***

I mentioned early on in this book that two of my biggest fears are the fear of failure and the fear of being judged. As an introvert and a highly sensitive person, those are hard fears for me to move through. I say "are" and talk about them in the present tense because to a certain extent, I will continue working on overcoming these fears for quite some time. And I want to remind you that your fears are valid, no matter how insignificant or stupid they seem to another person; they are valid. At one point in my life, these fears of mine manifested into the thought that I was not important or significant in any way; and to some people, I may not be.

On a planet with over seven billion people, living and creating their own reality, it is easy to get lost in comparison and to believe that there is nothing unique for one to contribute. But you have your own talents, your own passions, that you can share with the world or simply enjoy for yourself. Sure, there may be people who have similar interests, ambitions, talents, ideas, etc., but babe, none of them are *you*. So, quit sleeping on your dreams.

Writing out my story and sharing these insights with you does not make me or my ideas unique, but it does present them to you from a perspective that another person will never fully be able to understand. Take a moment after reading this paragraph and look up at what is in front of you. When you do, I need you to consider the fact that there is not another living being in this universe who will ever experience exactly what you are seeing, in the same way that you are—your perspective and the way you perceive is unique to you.

Questions to Contemplate:

1. **Where are my beliefs limiting my potential? How can I become more aware of these patterns? How can I change them or be more open-minded?**
2. **What is something I would do if I weren't afraid to try?**
3. **What do I value? In myself? In another person? In the world?**

20

CHAPTER TWENTY

I am on a journey to becoming more self-aware. I am unpacking the emotions and events of my past. I am building healthy habits that serve me in becoming the best version of myself. Now what? Where do you grow from here?

Every day we have the choice to try something new or repeat the patterns of the previous day. Making a real change in your life, especially when it deviates from the traditional, safe path, it can be difficult. It can be very scary, terrifying even. For me, I have learned to channel that fear into a different emotion, but wow, was that a fucking hard place to come to. There have been so many instances in my life where it has been tempting for me to follow the status quo, and in many ways, I have. But I have realized that keeping my sanity is far better than trying to keep the peace. Many distinguish their light for the sake of fitting in, and I understand why they do. Breaking the cycle is hard because it causes tension somewhere; and oftentimes, we feel that tension from the people closest to us.

There are times when you'll feel that tension within yourself, and *that* is what's scary because you begin to question if you chose the "right" path. Your mind runs wild, questioning every decision you make, bringing all of your insecurities to the forefront. *That* is the moment when you cannot give up on yourself. *That* will be the time when you need to cling to onto your faith, whether it be in yourself and/or in a higher power. *That* is when you are being challenged, and those emotions will keep coming up until you move through them.

Speaking from experience, there will be days when you question if you even want to pass those tests of life. I have never attempted or seriously thought of committing suicide, but I cannot lie and say that there haven't been thoughts that run through my head about what a world without me in it would look like, that there haven't been days where I question why I am still here on this earth. Those are scary thoughts to have. One of the hardest lessons for me to learn, and one that I don't think many people will easily accept is this: we are not our thoughts. If you are in a dark place, that is truly a difficult thing to believe, let alone remember. I understand that. I may not be able to resonate with what you are specifically going through, but I respect that it may be different.

What does that mean? *We are not our thoughts.* Living the human experience is an interesting thing to contemplate. I am alive, sitting here writing this book, but when you read it, I may not be. Who knows what year it is or what world you are living in when you get to this page. There have been several people who have written about and done research on "thoughts," what they are, where they come from, why we have them, and how much power they have. Candidly, I don't feel like I can properly articulate my own thoughts about "thoughts," but what I can say is this: they are powerful. They can be the greatest tool for guiding transformation in your life, but they can also be the wrecking ball that tears it all down.

So, where do you start? I will personally never stop recommending to people try meditation or journaling when they want to become more self-aware, but I understand that those practices can take time to get into a rhythm with. Side note, if you've tried to clear your head completely and not think about anything when you try meditating, that's not really the point. Instead, approach it with the intention of recognizing your thoughts as they pass through your mind. Allow them to float by, see them, sit with them for a moment or two, and then bring your attention back to your breath. As you build up your mental discipline, it will become easier to notice and question which thoughts are a response within yourself versus which ones stem from what you've been told or heard from other people.

When it comes to journaling, this is a practice that is so personal and different for each individual. Personally, I use the practice of journaling when I notice myself feeling super intense emotions or a numbness to them altogether. I have learned that both of those states are indications to myself that I need to get something out of my system rather than suppressing it and pretending it's not there.

The questions at the end of each chapter have been put there for you to poke your own buttons and draw out anything that you may not be aware needs uncovering. Take time to contemplate each of these questions and keep writing or meditating on them until you feel lighter—you'll know what I mean by "lighter" when you *feel* like there's nothing left to say.

After contemplating these questions and taking the time to look back on the events and experiences of your life, no matter

CHAPTER TWENTY

how seemingly insignificant, it is important to remember that while there may have been a lot that you wish would've been different, every single version of yourself in those moments got you to the person you are today; and the person you are today is going to get you to a future version of yourself.

***

Throughout this book, I have described how my vision has been a source of anxiety, and it has presented several challenges for me to overcome. While this is true, I also want to emphasize that, despite these challenges, I am no longer as insecure about as I was when I was a child. It is a unique aspect of my identity that literally impacts my perception. At times, I am extremely aware of my surroundings out of necessity because of it; and at other times, I can almost "tune out" things in the distance. I now perceive this disorder in a way that makes me value the importance of what is right in front of me, both literally and metaphorically. I am curious to see how my perception will change as I continue to get older, and I hope that one day, I will be able to describe it more articulately to others.

***

Looking back on the events and the experiences that have shaped me throughout the last 22 years, gratitude is what has kept, and continues to keep, me going. Gratitude for this moment is what makes life worth living. I look back on my past, and I think of the opportunities and the memories and the amazing experiences that I have already lived. The amount of joy, happiness, and gratitude that I have for those memories is what inspires me to share my story with you. It is what gets me out of bed and keeps me moving through my day. At one point, I didn't know that those experiences were possible or that some of those people even existed. That is what gives me hope for my future because I know that there are so many experiences that I have not had yet which will bring me so much joy and happiness to be immensely grateful for.

Life has its ebbs and flows. I know that each day will bring its own highs and lows; but now that I have shined a light on all of the shadows in my past, I know that they're there and will pop up every now and then. But the difference is, I know how to handle them better. When they do pop up, I know how to move through them without allowing them to control me. The most important thing that my eyes have been opened to throughout my life, is how important gratitude is. Because even when you have nothing left—when you *feel* like you have nothing left—gratitude is always a source of hope.

We are all born into this world innocent. With each day that passes, we are conditioned and conformed to function in the society around us. There may be members of our communities who struggle and suffer in ways that we'll never know for ourselves, but nonetheless, we all have our own challenges. We all have our own story. Who we become is the product of our circumstances, but most importantly, the choices we make in our lives. This book has been a conglomeration of all the choices, lessons, experiences, and people that have ever crossed my path in this life. It is simply one reflection of my perception of the world around me.

Long story short, I am a young adult trying to make sense of the world around me. You may not resonate with everything you've read in this book, but after closing it, you will move forward. Healing is not a linear path. Growth can look like taking two steps forward and three steps back. It can look like taking five steps forward and one step back. Progress is a process, and it looks different for everyone. When things get tough, hold on tight. Those are going to be the moments that you can learn the most from.

Thank you for coming along on this journey with me. I'm afraid it's time for our stories to part ways. I know that as I continue on my path, there will be even more difficulties ahead that are far more challenging than some of the stories I've shared in this book. However, I have hope for the future and I am looking forward to my next adventure. As I mentioned in the introduction, the memories I have shared here may one day not be as emotionally charged or significant as they are to me now. Nonetheless, they have been stepping stones on my journey. I will leave you with this final thought: your existence is creating a path that others may choose to follow in the footsteps of. You may even choose to follow in the footsteps of another. Regardless, at some point, we all deviate from the paths we follow to create our own. So, where do we go from here?

Questions to Contemplate:

1. **What am I grateful for? Make a list of at least 20 things.**
2. **When I imagine my life after healing from what I cannot change and letting go of what no longer serves me, what does my life look and feel like?**
3. **Write a letter to my older self. What do I hope to experience? What do I hope to learn?**

Citations

"Ghettos", *United States Holocaust Memorial Museum*, United States Holocaust Memorial
 Museum, https://encyclopedia.ushmm.org/content/en/article/ghettos. 15 October 2021.

Leave a Review!

What did you think of the book? What did you learn from contemplating the questions at the end of each chapter? **Let me know how you feel by leaving a review on Amazon:**

About the Author

Amanda E. Bjerke is a lifelong learner, teacher, and curious adventurer. She was born and grew up in a small town near Minneapolis, Minnesota and has since lived in Salzburg, Austria and Freiburg, Germany. When Amanda was a child, she was diagnosed with Ocular Albinism, an eye disorder that significantly impacts her vision. She received the Future K-12 German Teacher award by the National German Honor Society, Delta Phi Alpha, in 2020, and she is a 2021-22 Fulbright English Teaching Assistant. Her unique perception and passion for learning languages has guided her interest in communicating with people from different cultures and backgrounds about their individual human experiences.

When not writing or thinking, Amanda enjoys being surrounded by trees and the natural world, reading philosophy and romance novels, following her curiosity down the rabbit hole of YouTube, and dancing to music when no one is watching. She also spends her time connecting with her body and mind through yoga and meditation. *Opening Your Eyes: Becoming Self-Aware as a Young Adult in the 21st Century* is her first book.

You can connect with me on:
- https://linktr.ee/iamamandaevelyn

Subscribe to my newsletter:
- https://bit.ly/AmandaE-Newsletter

Made in the USA
Monee, IL
19 December 2021